GOOD

How to make sure that your child grows up right

J.P. VASWANI

Sterling Paperbacks

STERLING PAPERBACKS
An imprint of
Sterling Publishers (P) Ltd.
A-59, Okhla Industrial Area, Phase-II,
New Delhi-110020.
Tel: 26387070, 26386209; Fax: 91-11-26383788
E-mail: sterlingpublishers@airtelbroadband.in
ghai@nde.vsnl.net.in
www.sterlingpublishers.com

Good Parenting

© 2007, J.P. Vaswani

ISBN   978 81 207 3492 0

Published by Sterling Publishers Pvt. Ltd., New Delhi-110020.
Lasertypeset by Vikash Compographics, New Delhi.
Printed at Sterling Publishers Pvt. Ltd., New Delhi-110020

CONTENTS

YOUR TRUE WEALTH AND TREASURE

In my *yatras* to the East and West, I meet several old, well-known friends; and I make several new friends, too. They are indeed wonderful people, and many of them are doing great things, achieving success in different spheres of human activity. Yet others are struggling, working hard to achieve the same kind of success, with varying results. Almost all of them are busy amassing wealth!

There is nothing wrong with the pursuit of wealth. It was a wise man who said that wealth is an excellent thing, because it means power, it means leisure, and, above all, it means liberty to do what you like. All wealth too, as Locke says, is the product of hard work. I would, therefore, like to make it clear that I do not regard the pursuit of wealth as something wrong or immoral.

The point I wish to make is this: by all means accumulate wealth; but in the process, do not neglect your richest treasure – your children.

The other day I read that a collector had paid over a hundred million dollars for a painting at an art auction. Experts expressed the opinion that all of it was money well spent, because the 'investment' would repay rich returns in a few years' time: the price would almost double in 20-30 years, or so I was told.

How careful we are about our investments! How diligently do we not study the stocks and shares before we choose what we think is right for us! My only question to you is this: are you investing enough time and attention on your children, who represent your real wealth?

I recall the words of Gurudev Rabindranath Tagore who said, "Every child comes with a message that God is not yet discouraged of man." How true! Children represent the hope, the future, the possibility of salvation for all humanity. Or, as the poet Carl Sandburg put it so beautifully, "A child is God's opinion that the world should go on."

It is not without significance that one of the most sacred days of the Hindu calendar is the day of *Janmashtami* – the auspicious occasion when we celebrate the birth of the Divine Child, Bala Gopal, as he is fondly called by his *bhaktas*. On that day, pretty little cradles are seen in several Hindu households, with the image of child Krishna in them. The cradle is swung gently and songs are sung to Shyama, the Babe Divine of Brindaban.

And on the sacred Christmas day, Christians all over the world put out beautiful cribs with images of Baby Jesus therein. Is this not a testimony to the value that every culture, every religion places on the child?

Talking of Jesus, when his disciples asked him who was the greatest in the Kingdom of God, he called a little child unto him, set him in their midst and said to them: "Verily, I say unto you, except Ye become as little children, Ye shall not enter the Kingdom of Heaven. But he who humbles himself as this little child – he is the greatest in the Kingdom of Heaven!"

My Beloved Gurudev, Sadhu Vaswani, had wonderful things to say about the child and the child-heart:

The child is still a mystery to me. Does God come in the little ones to teach our hard and wayward hearts?

Children come with radiant faces and singing hearts. Do they not come to renew the child-heart that slumbers still in the grown-up ones?

Mystery-filled are the children, and radiant are they as stars. They come as witnesses to our Unseen Homes. In the eyes of a child floweth eternity: and in the heart of a child is the light that heals!

Philosophers have evolved systems and built up schools. But I know of no better touchstone for truth and falsehood than the child-heart!

Riches and glories of the earth pass away: but in the pure eyes and lisping words of a child may lie hidden, the wisdom that abides.

How eloquent - and how significant!

Suppose you were given a hundred-million-dollar painting: how safely would you guard it! Supposing you were given the world's largest diamond – how much care would you not take of it! And yet, the treasure that God has placed in your hands – your child – is greater than all of these! Alas!

Do you give your children the love and attention they deserve?

"But of course, we do, Dada," some of you may protest. "Do you know how much money we are spending on our children's care, clothes, education, toys, hobbies...?"

But that is not what I meant at all when I spoke of caring for your children! Money is not enough! Toys and games and fashionable, branded clothes and an expensive school are not all that a child needs. He needs your love, your friendship, your care, your guidance and discipline. He needs your loving attention so that he has the assurance that he is not alone, that there is someone who loves him dearly, someone whom he can turn to at any time of day or night.

I repeat, your children are your greatest treasure. Don't get so busy gathering silver and gold, that you neglect your richest treasure! Your children need your time, attention and love – for without love and attention, no child can grow up in the right way.

Today, parents are busy doing so many things. The father is a jet-setting executive, hopping across continents, playing golf at weekends, constantly talking on the cell phone at the dining table. As for the mother, she is a glittering socialite, the secretary of the exclusive Ladies' Club, attending coffee mornings, arranging kitty parties, visiting her beautician for extended sessions and spending the evenings at dinners, parties, concerts and ballets.

"Of course, we lead a busy and active life," these

parents will say. "But this does not mean that our children are neglected. They are provided with every comfort they need. They have their own specially designed bedrooms. We have a specially trained *ayah* / governess / babysitter to look after them. They have a car and a driver exclusively for their use and they are dropped at school and picked up from school. We have appointed servants to take care of their every need. And they *know* we love them!"

Many 'middle-class' parents fare no better. Juggling a double-shift between work and home, working mothers talk of spending "quality-time" with their children – a euphemism for very little time. As for the poor, they are struggling to feed the family, and they dare not talk of such luxuries as "quality-time".

Let me say to all parents – your children need your love, above all else. The nature of the soul is love – and without love, no child can grow up in the right way. You must give them your time! You must try to sow in their plastic minds seeds of character, without which life can have no meaning or value. You must help them to grow in the love and fear of God.

I recall the story of a young man in France. Having committed a heinous crime, he was sentenced to hard labour for ten years. He received his sentence calmly. But as he was being led away by the police, he turned towards the people present in court and shouted aloud so that everyone could hear him: "I have nothing against the judges – for they have dealt with me justly. I have nothing against the police – for they have done their duty. However, I can never forgive two persons in this courtroom – my father and my mother!"

People listened to him, shocked beyond words, too stunned to react.

"They are responsible for my present condition," he continued. "They paid no attention to my upbringing. They did not take care of the company I moved in; they never bothered to find out who my friends were. True, they gave me money to spend – but did not bother to find out what I spent it on. They did not object when I gambled, took to drinking and visited houses of ill-repute. And so here I am – full of vice and crime. The fault is theirs but I pay the price for it, sentenced to hard labour in prison, to be branded as a convict for life!"

Harsh words! But the young man's bitterness cloaks the truth that many parents do not seem to realize their responsibilities towards children.

The question then arises: "How should parents raise their children?" I offer you a few ideas, suggestions and practical tips in the pages that follow.

WHAT EVERY CHILD NEEDS

A world-weary gentleman once remarked, "I can't understand what all the fuss is about children. We are producing them in thousands every hour and yet people behave as if they are creating history whenever a baby is born!"

Parents are often overwhelmed by a sense of awe, wonder, mystery and deep love, when a new born baby comes into their lives. I dare say this is what parents have felt down the millennia, since human civilization dawned – but the wonder never ceases! There is a blessed sense of relief, a light-headedness that almost seems dizzy, and there is pure ecstasy when the little one is seen for the first time! And the thought arises in the mind of everyone who beholds a new-born baby – *I am witnessing the miracle of God's creation!*

All mothers are said to love their first-born best. The first children are, after all, the first miracles to stir within. They are the *originals*; the rest are, after all, modeled on the original. Everything is brand new about the originals – the gurgling, the crying, the smiles, the crawling, walking and teething. In their utter inexperience, the parents may be clumsy and overprotective – but the babies thrive, despite everything. As a wise mother puts it, the first-born are desperately wanted and loved.

When the second child is born, it dethrones the original and takes away from his elder sibling the title of 'only child'. By now, the parents are more relaxed, and actually begin to enjoy their baby. Of course, they've seen it all before – this one is *not* the first to gurgle, cry or smile. But he rises above it all.

It is not wrong to say that every mother loves her last child best – he revives the miracle of God in their lives! He makes his parents run around all over again, bringing youth and excitement back into their lives. By now, they are past masters at taking care of babies, so they throw caution and rules to the winds and just enjoy their new baby. But still, they feel that they are seeing one for the first time!

In the Hindu way of life, love and care for the child begins even when it is in the womb. Hindus strongly believe that the mother's state of mind, her living environment and her spiritual attitude during her pregnancy will influence the child in the womb. It is said that when Prahlada's mother was carrying him, she had been left in the care of Maharishi Narada. His constant chanting of the Name Divine, *Narayana, Narayana, Narayana,* so influenced the unborn child, that Prahlada was born a *Vishnu-bhakta,* despite being the son of the *Vishnu*-hating *asura,* Hiranyakashipu. We also know that Swami Vivekananda's mother was a great devotee of Lord Shiva, and earnestly prayed to Him to bless her with a divine child – and thus was born the great–souled Vivekananda.

Hindus believe that the mother-to-be must be surrounded by peace, calm, serenity and beauty; that she must hear and speak good, holy words and prayers; that she must think thoughts that are pure and noble – so that she may bring forth a child with these pure and noble qualities.

Hindu mothers are also enjoined to eat *sattvic* foods during pregnancy. They are discouraged from attending needless social gatherings such as parties and receptions, but urged to attend *satsangs*, visit temples, and participate in *bhajan*, *kirtan* and *naam-japa*. They are also enjoined to read holy scriptures and recite their prayers regularly. All these do's and dont's are meant only to ensure that the yet-to-be born child receives the best influences and the best vibrations even while he is in the womb. The young mother is constantly enjoined to remember that the little baby that she is moulding within her, is also an immortal soul – and her every word, thought and action will affect him.

I think it is very essential for parents to understand the various stages of development of a child, right from the time of his birth onwards. It is a human being who is being moulded, shaped by them, even as they themselves evolve as mature, responsible parents.

I'm afraid that many fathers are apt to imagine that they have *no* share of responsibility in bringing up their children. They believe that this is the mother's job – and hers alone. I have seen some fathers come and go as if they are visitors or boarders in their own houses, minding their own business, asking for their own needs to be attended to, and just favouring the baby with an occasional kiss and smile, taking no active interest in the welfare of their own children. If someone should protest about this, they cite the demands of their business as the reason for their neglect. Alas, they seem to forget that no amount of piling up of the earth's treasure, can compensate a man for the loss of those happy hours, when his children are growing up!

Remember too, that children are very different from adults. Children live in the *now*; they are free from the anxieties of the past or fear of the future. If your child demands your attention, give it to him then and there; don't give him an 'appointment' for tomorrow or later!

Every child is a human being, with a heart and soul. Never, ever let your child feel unwanted. Never forget, too, that every child is a unique individual, with his own personality and innate talents. Understand him and encourage him to express his creative potential. Guide him in a healthy, constructive way, to bring out the best in him.

Keep your child very close to yourself, until he is at least three years of age. He needs the affectionate touch of his mother, the loving smile of his father. It is a great blunder to hand little children over to the care of *ayahs* or babysitters.

That reminds me of a funny incident narrated to me. There was a young University student called Tom in the U.S. Being the eldest of several siblings, he had become an expert babysitter. When he entered college, his 'expertise' stood him in good stead, for his services were highly sought after, and earned him good money.

Once, a young mother had left her child in Tom's care with detailed instructions. She was delayed in her work and when she rushed back home, worried, she was amazed to find her little one out of his cradle, amusing himself happily in the playpen. He had been fed and wiped and cleaned.

"Oh, you're an angel," she said to Tom, with tears of gratitude. "You've changed his nappy too! Even his father won't do that!"

"Lady," said the young man, "I've been a mother much longer than you!"

One final word on the subject of babies: it is absolutely essential for mothers to breast-feed their new born children.

I am well aware that many mothers today do not want to do this, for reasons of their own. The milk that is produced in the mother's breast is the property of the infant – not the property of the mother. The mother who refrains from giving her milk to the child is actually stealing what belongs to the infant.

Nature has no judges, no courts, no policemen to arrest you for any wrong that you may do. Nature works in a simple way for setting wrongs right. It has been seen that children who receive milk from their mother's breasts, are the ones who revere and love their parents. While it is said that one of the causes of the growing incidence of breast-cancer is that the mothers have *not* fed their milk to the children.

When a child is born, the strong ties that bind him to his parents bring within their folds a heaven of happiness and excitement that they have never known until then. But this heaven is not without care, anxiety and pain – for love is not true love without sacrifice. And the parents must learn to *give* unselfishly, ceaselessly, unconditionally to the little one who depends on them for his very existence.

Every child that God sends out into this earth comes with infinite promise of love and joy and hope. But this can be realised, this promise fulfilled, only through love. Give your child the love and care and attention that he needs and he will grow up to be a wonderful human being who you will be proud of. Deny him the loving care he needs – and you will create a wayward child, a delinquent, a maladjusted adult. There is nothing better you can give your child than the pure, true love of your heart. This will make him *live* a good life and love you in return.

How To Be Good Parents

Many parents work hard to provide their children not only with basic necessities, but also with some of the luxuries of life. Toys and games to play with when they are kids; the best education possible; good clothes to wear, with jewellery thrown in for the girls; opportunity to study abroad, if that is possible; a lavish wedding; may be a flat or a bungalow for each; and property and land and stocks and shares to inherit...

Ajit was delighted when his children Ram and Radha were born. He adored his wife and loved his children deeply. He decided that he would work as hard as he could to build up his business, so that his family, especially his children would lack nothing that they needed or desired.

The children were put in the most exclusive – and expensive – international school in the city. But Ajit was never there for Parent-Teacher Meetings or the Annual Sports Day or Scholar's Day. His business engagements kept him away.

When his daughter expressed a desire to learn *Bharatnatyam*, the best dance teacher in town was engaged to teach her. While other girls wore simple costumes and artificial jewellery, he insisted that she should have nothing but silks and gold. But he was in Brazil signing a deal on the day of her *arangetram*. A diamond bracelet was hand-delivered to her before she went on stage.

When his son wished to play cricket, the bat, ball, pads and gloves were imported from England. When the young man was selected to represent his University, his father was in Delhi attending a Conference. But the son received a Rolex watch to mark the occasion.

Ajit wanted his daughter to take up Fine Arts at the University and become a famous dancer. He dreamt that his son would play for India one day.

At nineteen, the daughter decided to drop out of college and get married to the *tabla* player who had accompanied the musicians during her dance recitals. Ajit was broken-hearted.

After completing his B.A., his son decided that he would take up a diploma in catering and become a chef. Ajit was again rendered desolate.

"Why?" he asked repeatedly, confronting his children. "Why are you doing this to me? What is it that I have not given you? Is this the gratitude you show me for all that I have done for you?"

"We're not doing anything *to you*," his son said coldly. "We're simply doing what we want to do with our lives. We did not know that you gave everything to us with this price-tag attached – that we should live our lives as *you* want us to!"

"We did not want your *presents*, papa," the girl added for her part. "We wanted your *presence*. Where were you when we wanted to be with you?"

It is not that I'm telling you *not* to give presents to your children – but when you give them presents, hug them and kiss them and tell them you love them – this makes the presents more valuable. It's not that I'm telling you to spend every living and waking moment with your children – but even when you cannot be with them, continue to communicate your love and affection to them and ensure that they understand that your business and profits are *not* more important to you than they are.

Here are a few tips:

1) *Spend time with your children:*
Carry them around when they are infants; touch them, baby-talk to them, tickle them; run around with your toddlers; play hide-and-seek with your youngsters; take them out to parks, gardens, zoos and the seaside; spend holidays with them; teach them computer skills and car-driving as they grow older; be responsive to their evolving abilities and skills and make every activity with them an enjoyable game!

2) *Treasure every important event of their growing-up years:*
Collect photographs of the children at every stage of life; keep their art-work, their projects and their drawings safely preserved. On a birthday or other special days, sit down with the child and go through your collection – and the happy memories attached

to it. Birthday presents are always welcome – but they become unforgettable when the family gathers together to look at the child's 'Birthday Book of Memories'.

3) *Involve the child in your activities:*

The seven-year olds in Class III were asked to write a paragraph on the most exciting day they had spent that year. Some wrote about Deepavali celebrations; some spoke about the trip to the amusement park; little Tina wrote of the day she had spent with her dad, clearing the weeds from the garden and planting new seedlings. For her, it was "prime time" spent with her father – an unforgettable experience.

If you like to go for a quiet drive in the late evenings, take your child with you. If you like to watch the sunset from your terrace, keep your child by your side when you do it. If photography is your hobby, teach your child how the camera works and allow him to handle it. Take your child on your knee when you are working on your PC and show him how it works. Of course, your child cannot attend a business conference with you; or assist you to cook a banquet in your kitchen; but with a little modification, a little allowance, he can participate in your activities and feel 'grown-up' and 'important'.

4) *Give each child individual attention:*

Rajeev's overseas business partner was invited over for dinner. The burly American was delighted to meet Pinky, Rajeev's eight-year old daughter. "Hello, young lady," he beamed. "Which class are you in?"

"She's in class III now," Rajeev intercepted. Pinky's face fell; and the smile disappeared from her eyes. Her papa did not remember that she had been promoted just two months ago, and that she was now a 'big' girl in class IV!

A teacher gave her class a sentence-completion exercise to do. They had to complete the sentence beginning: "For me, happiness is…"

Nine year old Helen wrote: "For me, happiness is getting my feet wet on the seashore with mom – nobody else, but mom and me."

Devoting individual attention to a child is not always easy, especially when families are large, or when children are born too close to each other. But it's possible, with a little adjustment and lots of imagination!

The Kelkars have three growing children, Vishal(6), Varsha(5) and Varun(3). Every morning, it is papa's duty to get Vishal ready for school, and mama's, to see to Varsha. Varun is enlisted to help by being given important tasks like fetching didi's shoes and tasting dada's milk to ensure that there is sugar in it. If the parents are stressed or tensed about the day ahead, it is not communicated to the children. Everything is put on hold until Vishal and Varsha are safely seen off in the school bus. Then mama tells Varun, "Now we can relax, while papa gets ready for work."

Find time to talk to each child about his/her day; listen to them carefully as they narrate their 'adventures' at school; at all times make them feel that each one of them is the light-of-your-life, the apple-of-your-eyes.

5) *Surprise them with the unusual and the unexpected:*

By this, I do not mean just gifts. All I suggest is, don't let routine activities overwhelm your life. Don't get into ruts, doing the same things over and over again.

On Karan's tenth birthday, his father took him rowing at the local Boat Club, for the first time. Karan could never forget that day! He resolved that he would do exactly the same thing on *his* son's tenth birthday!

When your child asks, "Daddy, can I play with the garden hose?" or "Mummy, can I bake my own cake?" Don't come out with the stock "No!" For a change, say, "Why not?" And you will have made his/her day!

6) *Communicate with your child:*

Talk – listen – respond with understanding – express appreciation – show your disapproval. Whatever you do, however busy you may be, communicate with your child.

When your child nudges you, when he wants to talk to you urgently, *stop* whatever you are doing and listen to him with full attention.

The son of a famous writer was caught red-handed, stealing from his friend's locker, in a prestigious boarding school.

"You have brought shame upon your father," the Headmaster said to the boy sadly, when the boy was brought to him. "What will your father say when he hears about this shocking incident?".

The boy's voice quivered with emotion. "I know what he would say, 'Not *now* son, later!' This is what he always used to say to me whenever I went to him with a question or a bit of news – 'Not *now* son, I really haven't got time now. Come to me later.' Why should he say anything different now?"

So, listen to your child – but listen gently, kindly, lovingly. Do not interrupt the child; do not correct his pronunciation or his grammar when he is excited; do not mock him or belittle his concerns; don't argue with him or put him down when he is trying to open his heart to you, or share his ideas with you.

I know a family which has a large bowl on the dinner-table: it is the 'Talk-about-it' bowl. Each day, the children put in objects or drawings or clippings into it, about which they would like to talk during dinner. Each one enjoys having his/her turn to talk at the table, while the rest of the family listens.

Do not neglect to express your negative feelings: when a child says, "I want to run away," or "I don't like you," tell him/her, "I think you must be really angry." When they have been naughty or careless, tell them, "Mummy is very upset with you for leaving your room in a mess."

A contrite, "I'm so sorry!" or a soft "Mummy loves you!" is enough to smooth ruffled feelings, and all will end happily!

7) Offer possibilities to your child:

Show them that life is full of wonderful options. Tell them that there are opportunities galore awaiting them when they grow up. Do not limit their world and restrict their options. Read aloud to them when they are young; give them books to read – and you open up endless hours of delight. Play music for them and initiate them into the joys of appreciating one of life's finest pleasures.

Take them to visit art museums, natural landscapes, scenic hills and picturesque locations. As a parenting expert put it so beautifully, "Open doors for your child. Keep opening doors for them. They may not want to walk through every door you open. But just keep opening new doors and allow them to enter wherever they chose."

"Remember," he continues, "love does not spoil a child; too little discipline spoils a child. Love does not mean fostering dependence; or allowing wrong-doing; or showering a child with gifts; or bribing him with rewards to do what he must do; love means building a child's sense of self-esteem."

So, what are you waiting for? Start today! Love your child truly!

Parents Are Also Mentors
And Role-models

" The mother and the father are the deities whom we know first and foremost," proclaims a well-known Tamil proverb. *Mata, pita, guru, devo* – lists a saying from our ancient scriptures, placing parents even before God and guru. Sri Rama who is held up as the *Maryada Purushottam* – the ideal man of virtue and excellence, among all the *avataras* of Lord Vishnu – exemplifies what the *Puranas* call *pitru vakya paripaalana* – i.e. he who fulfills his father's commands. *Maatru devo bhava, pitru devo bhava* – your parents are the equivalents of Gods, the *Vedas* emphasise.

This is indeed a great honour! But this honour is to be *earned*, not just taken for granted!

Today, many parents complain that their children do not respect them and obey them. I would say to them: "Don't stop with complaints. Try a little introspection and see where things are going wrong."

Parents are not only their children's first and foremost teachers: they are also the children's role-models and mentors. If you want your child to be exceptional, you must also become exemplary role-models. As we all know, children are great imitators. They are extremely observant, attentive and sharp – and it is essential that we set a good example before them.

Three-year old Lisha was being taken to see her great aunt – her mother's eighty-year old *bua*. The old lady lived in a village, about two hours' drive from the city. Lisha's parents set out with her on a warm Sunday afternoon. The weather was so hot and dry, that they stopped for a cold drink at a stall outside the village.

"Aunty will be upset if she knows that we stopped here for a cold drink," said Amita, Lisha's mother. "So we'd better not tell her anything. O.K?"

"Shall I tell her that I had just one Limca?" enquired Lisha.

"No!" exclaimed her mother. "Just don't say *anything!* She's not going to ask you what you had to drink. So just keep quiet!"

"Should I tell her that I did not have a Limca?" Lisha asked. She was thoroughly puzzled.

"You stupid child!" scolded her mother, smacking the little girl's bottom. "Don't be so troublesome. Just keep quiet."

In about ten minutes, they were at the ancestral house where the old lady lived. Lisha's parents got down from the car and called Lisha to follow them. The child curled up in a corner of the back-seat and refused to move.

"I don't want to get down," she said. "I shall sit in the car. You both can see *bua*."

"But it's *you* she wants to see, not us!" her mother pleaded. "She's seen us any number of times! You are the special guest today. She's so eager to see you!"

"But I don't want to be seen," Lisha said stubbornly, clinging to her corner.

"Now that's enough," said her father, trying to pick the child up and carry her out of the car. But Lisha let out such a loud howl that he hastily put her back. He knew that she could be inconsolable, unmanageable if she started howling.

Begging, pleading, coaxing, cajoling, nothing worked. "Alright then," said Amita, through clenched teeth, "you can sit and cook in that hot, uncomfortable car, while we go in and sit in *bua's* cool, comfortable parlour."

Just five minutes later, they returned with the old lady, who was not ready to accept their excuses. "How could you leave the poor child in the car?" she had scolded. "I shall get her inside."

With difficulty, the frail old lady climbed down the porch steps and came round to the back door of the car. "So you are my great niece Lisha?" she said to the little girl. "Aren't you a pretty little princess? Let's have a look at you!"

Promptly, Lisha covered her face with her hands and buried her head in her knees.

"What have I done now?" coaxed the old lady gently. "Don't you like me? Wouldn't you like to come and see the big house where your mother was born and brought up?"

"No, I wouldn't," mumbled the child.

"I've been waiting to see you," the old lady pleaded. "Why are you angry with me? I've made *gulab jamoons* and ice-cream with jelly especially for you..." Here, the old lady wiped away an imaginary tear. With a little sob, she said, "And you say you won't even come in to see this old *bua*..."

Lisha raised her tear-stained face from her knees and put her arms around the kind old lady's neck. "I love you *bua*," she sobbed. "I really love you, but I had a Limca to drink. I'm sorry, I'm sorry," she sobbed. "I had a Limca to drink."

Lisha's parents exchanged guilty looks. Their hypocritical injunctions to the child had upset her so much that she had preferred to stay in the car, rather than come out and utter lies to her aunt or displease her parents by speaking the truth. What was a bit of falsehood for them, was an impossible situation for the child!

Children look up to their parents as living examples. Teachers and elders tell a boy, "You must not smoke. It is a bad habit and can harm you." The boy sees his father smoking. He says to himself, "People tell me smoking is bad, but papa seems to be enjoying it. I think I shall also smoke when I grow up."

Examples speak louder than words!

The best discipline is self-discipline. Unless parents have self-discipline and self-control, they cannot expect their children to be disciplined.

Discipline is not merely refraining from bad habits and addictions like smoking, drinking and gambling. It is also a matter of adhering to ethical values and morals in deeds of daily living. At work, at home and in company, make sure that you never compromise on your principles and values.

Parents should also carry out their daily spiritual practices regularly, before their children. This might be assembling for morning or evening prayers; conducting a brief *pooja* at home; having a little *kirtan* session; reading aloud from the scriptures; or just sitting in silent meditation. By carrying out such practices, we emphasise the value of faith, prayer and meditation in the minds of the little ones.

In some families, children are taught to say a few prayers as soon as they learn to speak. While other families teach them to utter the Name Divine. This is one of the best gifts you can give your children. Faith will come to them spontaneously, and the power of the Lord's Name will stand by them in their darkest hours – and they will surely thank you for bestowing the great gift of Faith on them!

In order to live wholesome, harmonious, meaningful lives, there are other virtues that must be inculcated in children – virtues such as patience, tolerance, compassion, forgiveness and understanding. These virtues cannot be imbibed through sermons or lectures – but when they see *you* practising them, the children will adopt them readily and willingly.

Little Rohan's parents engaged the services of a young girl to look after him. The girl's name was Sangeeta, and she had been sent out from the village to earn a little money to support her impoverished family.

Rohan's parents treated Sangeeta very harshly. They constantly scolded her and berated her; they criticised everything she did; and they spoke rudely and harshly to her.

When Rohan entered kindergarten, his teacher was horrified to hear the language he used with his friends. "You stupid, clumsy fool!" he would yell. "Don't just stand there! Make yourself useful!" It was exactly the kind of language that his parents used to speak to Sangeeta!

There is a parable told us of a very rich lady, who lived right next door to a very poor lady with three children.

It happened that one day, the poor woman had nothing, not even a loaf of bread to offer her hungry children. Humbly, she went to the door of the rich lady and said, "Can I have just one loaf of bread to give my children, who are starving?"

"I'm sorry I have no bread left even for myself," lied the rich lady. "How can I give *you* a loaf?"

"Please look carefully," pleaded the poor woman. "I'm sure that you must have a little bit of bread somewhere in your cupboard."

"No I don't," snapped the rich lady. "There is no bread in my cupboard."

"But you are so rich, that it cannot be!" cried the poor lady.

"If there is any bread in my cupboard, may God change every bit of it to stone," swore the rich lady. "Now please go, because I have nothing to offer you."

When the poor lady had left, with tears in her eyes, the rich woman turned to her children and said, "Let's eat in peace now."

The soup was set on the table. The butter was brought out, and the lady went to get bread from the cupboard. She was shocked to discover that it had indeed turned into stone.

"Mama, mama," cried the children. "We are hungry."

"Don't worry," said the rich woman. She gave a five pound note to her servant and ordered her to buy three fresh loaves from the bakery.

When the servant returned, she found that she could not lift the basket containing the bread. She opened the basket to find that three piping hot loaves which the servant had got from the bakery, had turned to stone the moment she touched the basket.

She was shocked. She ran to the bakery and brought bread and cakes for her poor neighbour. For good measure, she bought plenty of provisions from the grocery store.

"Here you are sister," she said breathlessly; as she handed over the gifts. "I have learnt a bitter lesson today: I will never ever be selfish."

When she returned home, the stones in the basket turned into bread. The children ate hungrily. They learnt that they had to be generous to everyone around them.

WHEN DOES A CHILD'S EDUCATION BEGIN?

A ristotle was the most respected teacher in Athens. The city's best and brightest young men gathered around him at his Lyceum to receive an all-round 'liberal' education, aimed at making them ideal citizens and ideal human beings.

Once, a young mother approached Aristotle. She dreamt of the day when her little son would become Aristotle's student. In her eagerness she wanted the boy to be prepared for it right from his childhood.

"When should I begin training my child, so that he may grow up to be an ideal human being?" she asked the great teacher.

"How old is your child?" enquired Aristotle.

"He is barely five now," said the eager mother.

"Waste no more time, dear lady," said Aristotle, "You are already five years late."

It is never too early to start inculcating values in your children!

Many parents are beginning to feel that their children are drifting apart from them and the rest of the family. They also feel that their children are beginning to lose respect for the ancient Indian values and ideals they cherished. For such parents, I recommend a 5-point programme:

1) Everyday, all the members of the family – from the youngest to the eldest – should spend a little time in prayer together. As the saying goes, 'the family that prays together, stays together'. At such sessions, a thought from the scriptures or an inspirational book should be read and each and every member must be asked to offer his or her reflections on that thought. This gives everyone a sense of involvement in the prayer and makes the prayer personal rather than mechanical.

2) Parents must realize that the mother is the greatest influence in the life of a child – especially during the formative years, when the child is in the impressionable, moulding stage. It is under her influence that the child's character is shaped. By the shining example of her life, she can infuse in the children love for their cultural heritage, traditions and values, so that the children will always know where their roots are.

3) The father too, has an important role to play. Whatever may be his business pre-occupations, he must spend as much time as possible with his children everyday. He should go out with his family during weekends, and on brief holidays at least twice a year.

4) The TV must cease to be the focus of the family in the evenings. The dominant place given to the TV

in our homes truly distresses me. In all their free time, the children's eyes are glued to the TV screens. Not only does this have a harmful effect on their eyes, but also makes them sluggish and lethargic. What is worse, the impact of the violence and other undesirable elements shown on the TV makes an indelible negative impression on young minds. The TV must be displaced, substituted with some other healthy, creative pastime for the children.

5) Children should be enrolled in weekly classes where they could be introduced to and taught the essentials of India's deathless culture. This is especially important for Indian children who live abroad. They should be made to realise that even though they live far away from their homeland, they belong to India, and feel proud about being inheritors of a rich, immortal, culture and tradition, which is regarded as the light and hope of a decaying world.

LOVING DISCIPLINE

How should parents raise their children?
By proper precept, guidance, patience and loving discipline.

Without discipline, no art can be learnt – and definitely not the art of living.

In the 1960's and '70's, 'discipline' was regarded as a dirty word. The cult of 'self-expression' was fashionable. People used to say, "Don't restrain your child. Don't discipline him. Let him express himself freely." And so, children, especially in the affluent west, were allowed to do as they pleased. Even infants had their 'freedom'; they were fed only when they cried – and not as per a regular time-schedule. Child-specialists called this 'demand-feeding'! Children were not scolded or reprimanded; they were allowed 'to be themselves'.

But what kind of 'self' is that which seeks free expression and defies discipline? Surely, it is not the higher self in the being. Such 'freedom' leads not to license, but to licentiousness; it feeds and waters the lower self, the ego – the self of desire and unruly passions, of cravings and animal appetites. When a

31

child is indulged and allowed to surrender to his whims and fancies, he begins to kick tantrums, he loses his temper and behaves as he pleases.

Sometime ago, I received an American newspaper carrying the headline: *School-gang violence is now near-epidemic: vandalism, arson, murder, burglary.* The paper quoted an official of the Los Angeles County Board of Supervisors, who said: "We *have* to return to discipline! Without discipline in the home, we are not going to have it in the schools or on the streets. We must arouse public opinion for a change." The paper also reported how three teenagers – aged fourteen, fifteen and seventeen – had killed a man and a woman just to steal from them a paltry sum of three dollars and ten dollars!

In subsequent years, the world was shocked to hear of school boys or college students just opening fire on their friends and teachers on the campus, causing needless bloodshed and loss of lives – apparently, without any reason!

You might respond to this by saying, "But Dada, surely we have also heard that in India too, a harsh word from the teacher, or a stern beating by the headmaster, have led some sensitive young students to commit suicide! Is not such 'discipline' terrible?"

Let me explain to you – discipline is necessary; discipline is vital. But discipline must not be confounded with suppression or oppression.

A friend said to me that when he had been transferred to one of India's metros, he and his wife began to hunt for a good school for their only child, a daughter. They were told that such-and-such a school was the 'ultimate' institution for girls in the city, and went to visit the school. It was situated in beautiful, green environs, and the atmosphere was serene and still – and silent!

"Is today a holiday?" the wife inquired of the watchman at the gate.

"No madam," he said. "Classes are going on."

"When will the children be out?" the lady asked. "I'd like to see their uniforms… and may be, have a word with them?"

"You will find two classes out in the sports field," the man said. "They are having their PT and sports now. If you go through the main building and pass the Assembly Hall, you will reach the playground."

The parents walked down the neat path. On either side were lawns and well laid-out gardens. "Students are not allowed to step on the lawns," a red-and-white notice warned.

They entered the main building and were impressed by the elegant marble foyer with its vast reception area. "Students not allowed beyond this point," said another notice.

They crossed the visitors' area and walked down a long corridor that led to the back of the building. "Students must walk in single file on the left," said another notice.

They passed by a vast library. "Students are not permitted to go beyond the counter," said another notice at the entrance.

At the back of the main building was a huge playground. On the far side, a class was engaged in a drill. On the near side, another class was playing a group-game. One girl stood aside, obviously having gotten 'out' of the game.

"Hello, honey," said the lady to her. "What is your name?"

The child turned to her spontaneously and said, "Hello aunty…" and stopped short. A look of fear crossed her eyes. "Excuse me," she mumbled, and ran away!

Another girl came 'out' and the lady smiled at her. "How do you like your school, dear?"

The child cast a furtive glance all around and whispered under her breath, "Sorry aunty! We're not allowed to talk to anyone." And she turned her face away.

The parents were bewildered. They returned thoughtfully to the car. "I don't think I want Shweta to come here," said the mother, shortly. "The children don't even *talk* or *laugh*! And wherever you turn, there are warnings and restrictions. How can any child be happy here?"

Discipline must not be confounded with suppression.

There was a little boy. When someone asked what his name was, he answered, "Haresh Don't".

"Don't?" said the visitor. "That's a strange surname. Are you sure you are Haresh *Don't*?"

"Sure, I'm sure," said the boy solemnly. "Every time I want to play in the house, mama says, 'Haresh,

34

don't!' Every time I laugh loudly, papa says, 'Haresh, don't!' Every time I run down the stairs, someone says, 'Haresh, don't!' So my name is *really* Haresh Don't."

This is not the kind of discipline I am talking about. We must treat our children like the intelligent beings that they are. We must teach them about the values that are essential to them; we must tell them about the gift of human life and explain to them that discipline is needed to reach life's goals.

THE RIGHT KIND OF DISCIPLINE

Our mothers taught us through precept and example. They narrated to us wonderful stories from the ancient scriptures. Grandmothers told children about Rama and Sita, Krishna and Radha, Kansa and Duryodhana, Ravana and Hiranyan-kashipu. They took great care to indicate how life might be lived in the right way, by devoting our energies to the service of certain high ideals. The Epics and the *Puranas*, the lives of the great *avataras* of the Lord, heard in the years of childhood, left an indelible impression upon our minds.

Have you seen some boys and girls stand up courteously whenever an older person enters the room? Have you seen some children gladly offering their seats to older people on the bus or in a crowded hall? Such courtesy is ingrained in them by the examples set before them by their parents.

All discipline must be blended with love, so that the child has the assurance that it is for his own benefit, and not in obedience to blind, arbitrary 'rules'. I do not believe in the old-fashioned saying, "Children should be *seen* and not *heard*." I think the sound of children's laughter and their tinkling voices are among the most melodious sounds on earth. This is perhaps why the Tamil Poet-Saint, Thiruvalluvar, wrote: "They say that the flute and the lyre are sweet – that is, those who have not heard the beautiful prattling of their own children."

Don't laugh – don't play – don't talk loudly – these are superficialities. Do not restrict your children by unnecessary rules and regimentation. Rather, set examples before them. The child learns more through example than preaching.

As a child, Sadhu Vaswani was sitting in his class one day, when a pleasant, playful thought crossed his mind. The child's eyes lit up and a beatific smile played upon his lips. The class-teacher, who must have been a harsh, unimaginative man, slapped the child sharply.

I am sure the child must have been shocked and hurt. But, as he said to us much later, there and then he made up his mind that when he grew up, he would start a school where young children would be treated with love, affection and reverence, and no physical punishment would ever be meted out to any of them; a school where the teacher would be a *friend*, rather than a task-master.

Sadhu Vaswani was lucky enough to actually get into such a 'model' school very soon; he was enrolled in Sadhu Hiranand's Academy and benefited greatly from learning at the feet of a great-souled teacher who was not only a friend, but a preceptor and a role-model whom he would revere throughout his life.

Today, in the numerous schools founded under the umbrella of Sadhu Vaswani's *Mira Movement in*

Education, we happily spare the rod — in fact, we do very well without it; but I'm glad to say, we do not spoil our children – witness the bright, happy children in our schools and the young adults who always return to their *alma mater* as they would to their parental homes.

"I never, ever beat my child, Dada," a young mother assured me. "Whenever she is naughty, I lock her up in her room for half an hour. Believe me, she learns her lesson that way!"

You can imagine my reaction to this method of 'discipline' – I was horrified!

Many parents don't seem to have the right notion of 'discipline'. Some of them resort to hitting, slapping and pulling the ears. Others resort to psychological punishment by refusing to talk to the child or even look at him. Yet others issue threats and dire warnings. Some resort to constant nagging and verbal abuse.

All this will only frustrate your child and make him defiant.

Discipline is necessary – for children are in the learning stage and their parents are their first and foremost teachers. But love and discipline should go together.

An old man was taking a walk with his grandson in the wood, when they came across a small land turtle.

The boy eagerly picked it up to examine the creature closely. To his utter dismay, the turtle promptly pulled in its head. No amount of prodding or pushing would bring its head out.

The grandfather took the turtle and said to the little boy, "Don't hurt him. You can't force him to do something that he doesn't want to do."

They took him home and the grandfather placed the turtle near the roaring log-fire in the living room.

In a few minutes, the turtle stuck out its head and slowly began to move towards the boy.

"Never try to force a fellow into anything," said the wise old man. "Just warm him with a little kindness and he will respond positively."

Practical Suggestions

- Give your children your attention when they are well-behaved and happy. They must not get the idea that they get 'noticed' only when they are naughty.

  Reshma was delighted when her friend, Preeta came to visit her after a lapse of several years. Dumping a few toys before her young son Mahesh, Reshma began to exchange gossip with her friend.

  In about ten minutes, Mahesh got tired of playing on his own. Slowly, he crept up to his mother and nudged her gently.

  "Mama, mama," he called. "Come and play with me."

  Too involved in her gossip even to turn around and look at him, Reshma simply pushed his little hand away and continued her conversation.

  When the nudging became more insistent, Reshma turned to her son with an upraised finger and said, "Shh!" A look of warning flashed in her eyes.

For a few minutes, Mahesh subsided – but only for a few minutes. Shortly, he climbed up on the sofa between his mother and her friend, jumped up and down on the velvet cushions, screaming, "Mama! Mama!"

"You naughty boy," said Reshma in exasperation. She lifted him up from the sofa and deposited him back on the floor. "Be a good boy now – and, here you are, you can play with the telephone – you like the phone, don't you? Talk to your *naana* and *naani*." And the cordless handset was thrust into his hands as a 'present' for his promised good behaviour.

Mahesh was delighted with the phone – for exactly five minutes, during which time he had made imaginary calls to his papa, his grandparents and several others. At the end of five minutes, his attention turned to his mother. Why wasn't she looking at him? Why wasn't she talking to him – playing with him?

Mahesh looked at the cordless handset and then at his mother. Then he flung the handset on the centre-table; the glass top of the table cracked and a flower vase fell off the table, spilling water on the expensive Persian carpet.

"MAHESH!" screamed his mother in exasperation. Her friend was forgotten; her gossip was forgotten; she strode angrily towards the child and picked him up in her arms, scolding him – but Mahesh's purpose had been served: his mama *had* eventually left her friend to notice *him* and pay attention to *him* !

Child psychologists call this behaviour "attention-seeking-syndrome." The child begins to feel that he will not be 'noticed' if he is quiet and well-behaved, whereas a bit of mischief will immediately bring him all the attention he needs!

- Ensure that your child gets your attention for good behaviour. Even if you are busy, notice him and praise him for being well-behaved.
- Ensure that 'rules' for good behaviour are mutually accepted by you and your children. Also, let children understand the consequences of breaking rules – like being taken away from visitors, not allowed to touch gadgets, not being given biscuits, chocolates, etc.
- Always be consistent in applying rules. For instance, if a child is not allowed to walk out of the front door on his own, the rule is permanently applicable. He cannot be permitted to walk out alone, just because you are engrossed in your TV programme, or chatting to your friend on the phone.

With older children, especially teenagers, the 'rules' are obviously more stringent.

- There should be strict monitoring of the TV viewing. The violence and immorality depicted in some programmes can be the ruin of young minds.
- It is equally important to curb 'browsing' on the internet. The stories of crimes generated by such mindless surfing are quite horrible.

I understand there are electronic devices to prevent teenagers from watching certain channels and accessing certain websites. I think such 'censorship' is essential for youngsters no matter what the advocates of 'freedom' have to say!

- Parents should also be aware of their teenaged children's 'friends'. They must ensure that children do not get into bad company and fall a prey to bad habits.

    It is a good idea to permit your children to bring their friends home once in a while, even if you are too busy to 'entertain' them. Do spare the time to talk to them and get to know their friends. Make their favourite snacks; organize a little party when you can; get to know about their backgrounds; get in touch with their parents.

- Excessive 'pocket money' is not at all a good idea! Children must be taught that money is to be *earned*, not merely squandered. Above all do not fall into the trap of offering cash as a 'reward' or 'incentive' for induced behaviour.

- It is a good idea to send children to special *yoga* or meditation groups with children of their age. These disciplines inculcate will power and spiritual strength.

- Do not pamper your children with needless luxuries. They should be exposed to the rough and the smooth, to rain and sunshine. As they grow, they should be encouraged to look after themselves, polish their shoes, clean their rooms and make their beds.

- Temper tantrums and bad behaviour should be ignored, rather than 'noticed' or 'attended' to. Let the anger and violence subside and then make the child understand that such behaviour is not acceptable. But do talk to them and try to understand the cause of their frustration. In other words, ignore negative behaviour until the 'bad mood' passes – and then talk to the child when he is in a positive, receptive frame of mind.

The following list of ten cannots is attributed to Abraham Lincoln. You can instil these in your children too! But of course, you will have to imbibe them yourself first, before you can expect them to learn the same!

- You cannot bring about prosperity if you discourage thrift.
- You cannot strengthen the weak by weakening the strong.
- You cannot help 'small' folk by treading down 'big' folk.
- You cannot lift up the wage-earners by pulling down the wage-payers.
- You cannot help the poor by destroying the rich.
- You cannot make ends meet if you spend more than you earn.
- You cannot bring about peace by creating quarrels among men.
- You cannot establish security on borrowed funds.
- You cannot build character and courage if you take away initiative and independence.
- You will never help anyone by permanently doing for them what they could and should do for themselves!

Make A Heaven Of Your Home!

There was a little boy who longed to visit the very edge of the world, where he believed, heaven and earth met. Often, as he sat at the window of his humble cottage, he could see the horizon where the sun set, and it seemed to him that it was so beautiful!

One day, with his eyes firmly fixed on the horizon where the earth and heaven seemed to meet, he set out to get there. He walked on and on; he seemed to have lost his way as evening came, and found himself in a valley, where the horizon was no longer visible.

Dispirited and tired, he knocked at the door of a cottage. A kind woman opened the door. He told her of his quest and begged her to direct him to the place where heaven met earth.

"There it is," she said, pointing to a spot at a distance. "But do hurry, for it will soon be dark."

The boy hurried up the slope of a hill following her directions, and all of a sudden, he was at the door of his own home, where his mother stood smiling, with open arms, to receive him. And, just in front of his doorstep was the magnificent view of the horizon, where the sunset presented a glorious sight.

"My own home," the little boy thought to himself. "Now I know this is the place where heaven and earth meet!"

Truly, it has been said that the home is the door to the Kingdom of God, the Kingdom of true happiness. But you cannot just buy or rent a heaven-like home ready-made and offered to you for the asking! As parents, it is *you* who can turn a brick-and-mortor house or dwelling into a *home* where faith and mutual understanding flourish.

Needless to say, the mother's role is vital in making the home heaven-like. It is her nature, her qualities, her temperament which will go to build her home and influence her children. It is her personality which is stamped upon the home she lives in – and the family she raises.

The distinguished French politician and Foreign Minister, Robert Schuman, was once asked why he had never married.

"I made up my mind not to marry a long time ago," he replied. "I was travelling on the metro once. The train was crowded and accidentally, I stepped on an elegant lady's foot. Before I could even open my mouth to apologize, she let off such a hideous stream of abuse, that I was stunned – and all this, without even looking back at me! 'Idiot, clumsy oaf!' she swore, 'can't you see where you are putting your foot?' Then she glanced at me and she went red with embarrassment. 'Oh please forgive me, monsieur,' she cried in a sweet, pleading voice; her entire demeanour had changed. 'Do forgive me, I thought it was my husband!'

"If that is the way ladies treated their husbands," he concluded, "I thought I was better off staying single!"

Married women will say that this is a one-sided anecdote to illustrate the point; and I agree with them; it is equally up to the men, to help their wives make the home a happy, harmonious haven for the children to grow up.

The word for the married state in our ancient Sanskrit language is *grahasta ashrama*. Marriage is considered as an *ashrama* – a place of discipline: *not* a pleasure hunting ground. Marriage is not a license. It is at once a discipline and a responsibility.

In a happy and successful marriage, a husband and wife should love and respect each other, to bring out the best in each other. They should help each other to grow in the spirit of love, understanding, forgiveness and selflessness. They should support each other to evolve and unfold their highest potential. If this is kept in focus as the goal of marriage, love and harmony will surely prevail in the home.

Here is a beautiful prayer that I came across in a book:

Let there be harmony between husband and wife.
Let there be harmony between parents and their children.
Let there be harmony among different relatives.
Let there be harmony among friends.
Let there be harmony among the elements.

Let there be harmony between the earth and the sky.
Let harmony be experienced everywhere!
May God bless you with harmony and peace!

Above all, parents must realise that children are not their 'toys' or 'personal achievements'; nor are they your future insurance. They are souls whom God has entrusted to your care. You are not expected to pamper or indulge them mindlessly; rather, you must blend firmness with affection, discipline with love, to give them a secure and healthy environment where they might grow to absorb the deeper values of life.

Humility and understanding are the keys to harmony and happiness in the home. When parents learn to love and appreciate each other and their children, then familial bonds are strengthened.

To understand is to stand under! Therefore, understanding helps you to grow in the spirit of humility. Unfortunately, humility has become a rare virtue these days. Nobody wants to stand *under* anyone – everyone wants to stand above everyone else – no wonder then, that the divorce rate is increasing and homes are breaking! Parents say they cannot understand their children; children claim that they cannot understand their parents.

"Why should we stay at home and look after the children?" young women argue. "Let our husbands do the cooking, cleaning and child-minding!"

"Why on earth should I help with the children and the house work?" husbands want to know. "I bring in the money, so I will not lift a finger in my own home!"

I would call for a little more empathy among marriage partners. Empathy is nothing but understanding the other person's point of view. The golden command, do-as-you-would-be-done-by is a splendid instance of empathy. It is an excellent technique for strengthening marriage bonds and making the home a happy haven.

I urge young people to enter into marriage with a serious sense of commitment, integrating head and heart. It is a commitment one makes for a lifetime and not to be taken lightly. When you enter marriage with this sense of commitment, your home is sure to become a temple of love, peace, joy and harmony – a centre of light amidst the encircling darkness. The love and peace that emanates from such homes reaches out, radiates towards others. The parents and children from these homes have the wonderful ability to love and serve others and can become the catalysts who transform society.

CHILDREN ARE NOT ADULTS!

Have you witnessed a children's Fancy Dress competition? Little boys and girls 'dress up' not only as Krishna, Radha and Mother Mary, but also parade before us solemnly as Mahatma Gandhi, Mother Teresa, Pandit Nehru and Netaji Subhash Chandra Bose.

Everyone watches the little ones utter a few 'words of wisdom' attributed to the great souls – and everyone, without exception, claps and cheers. The little ones do steal our hearts, and we go, "Ah...!" "Ooh...!" "How cute!" and so on.

There was a little girl who put on the role of *Jhansi Ki Rani* at such a show. She drew thundering applause from the crowd as she squeaked in her childish vioice, *"Meri Jhansi nahi doongi!"* ("I shall never give away my Jhansi!") But hardly had the claps died when she tripped on her wooden sword and fell face down on the stage. Jhansi was forgotten; and the role-play was forgotten as a frightened, hurt, four-year old cried out, "Mummy, mummy, I've fallen!"

In a town-bus, packed to capacity, a small boy stood among a crowd of adults, holding carefully onto a scrap of wood. He had a tough time making sure that the jostling crowd of passengers did not knock the scrap off his hands.

A lady who had been observing him for sometime, couldn't bear the suspense for any longer. "Why are you holding so carefully onto that little scrap?" she asked him, raising her voice above the roar of the engine.

He turned to her and replied earnestly, "I'm taking Lucy for a ride. She's my friend, and this is her first trip on a bus."

"But...but where's Lucy?" the lady asked, bewildered.

"Look carefully," said the little boy, drawing her attention to the scrap of wood. "Lucy is a little ant. I found her in my garden and she is now my best friend!"

How imaginative, how kind – and how sweet, innocent and childlike!

It was Jesus Christ who said to us that we cannot enter the kingdom of Heaven unless we become like little children!

A renowned doctor was busy in his study, when his small son came into his room and stood silently by the table. Not wishing to be disturbed, the doctor put his hand into his pocket and drew out a dollar-bill and offered it to the boy.

"But I don't want any money, daddy," said the lad.

Growing a little impatient, the doctor snapped, "Well, what *do* you want?"

"I don't want anything," said the boy. "I only want to be near you!"

We are adults; it is we who must try to understand the children's needs.

Young mothers know that babies cry most of the time; but they don't always know why the baby is crying! It's not just because they are hungry. It may be that they are afflicted with colic-pain due to indigestion. It may be that they are developing a fever or some infection. It may even be that they are very tired and have to be rocked to sleep, or soothed, calmed down with a lullaby.

Parents teach their children to walk and talk. They show the children what is what, and teach them to recognize dogs, cats, butterflies and flowers. But parents must also learn to understand the child's needs and anxieties and fears and aspirations!

Six year old Ravi was playing out in the garden with his friends. His mother had to go down to the neighbourhood store for some urgent purchase. She locked the house and gave the key to Ravi before she left.

When she returned ten minutes later, Ravi was still playing in the garden.

"Give the keys back to me Ravi," she called.

Ravi came running up to her. "It's safe in my pocket, Ma," he said, and put his hands into the pocket of his shorts. He fumbled, and began to frown, twisting his hand inside his pocket, trying to locate the key.

"Come here," said the mother impatiently. "Let me look."

She put her hand into his pockets, and was appalled at the stuff that she found!

There was a little piece of string, a shiny pebble, a piece of fluffy cotton, an empty blue bottle, a chocolate wrapper – and even a withered leaf!

"Look at all the rubbish!" the mother scolded angrily. "Where is my key?"

Fortunately, the key was safe in the other pocket. Along with the key, a little bell fell out.

"What a funny boy you are!" laughed the mother, relieved to have found the key. "What is this bell for?"

"It's a magic bell brought from the bottom of the sea!" said Ravi, with shining eyes. "If you ring it, happiness will come to you and sadness will go away."

"Oh yes?" said the mother. "And who told you about this bell?"

"I found it on the road," said Ravi, "and a little caterpillar lying next to it told me all about it."

To the mother, all the stuff in Ravi's pocket might have seemed like rubbish. But to the child's imagination, each object was precious! How hard it is for adults to understand children! And how patient children have to be when they face adult intransigence!

A little boy was holding a sparrow with a broken wing. A kind lady saw him sitting solemnly on the park bench, stroking the wounded bird.

"Sonny, would you like me to take this sparrow home and nurse it back to good health?" she asked him gently.

She assumed that the boy was feeling sorry for the bird, but didn't know what to do with it.

"I promise you I will bring it back here when it is healed," she continued. "Together, we will let it free again."

The little boy thought for a moment. Then he said to her, "Thank you Ma'am. But I would like to take care of the bird myself." He paused, and then added, "You see, I can understand this bird better."

The lady was about to protest, when she saw the boy rise up. Then she realized that the boy was lame. His left leg was in a caliper!

"Did you say your prayers last night?" the parish priest asked little Belinda.

"Well... sort of," was her reply.

"What do you mean?" said the priest sternly. "We have taught you to pray properly in Sunday school, haven't we?"

"Well," said Belinda. "I went down on my knees and began to say my prayers – then I thought God must be tired of listening to the same old prayers day after day. So I got into bed and told him the story of the three little pigs instead."

Children want love and attention and time from their parents – not just toys and chocolates and gifts and dresses and money!

True, we have to work hard to provide for the future of our children; true, we must make sure that their material needs are met. But children have other needs too, and we must not fail to fulfill them.

"Mummy, please play with me," begged little Deepa. Her mother was busy at the computer, preparing a project report for her boss.

"Not now honey," she said to Deepa. "Mummy is very busy now."

"Why are you always so busy?"

"Because I have lot's of work to do."

"Why do you have to work so much?"

"So that I can earn lots of money for us."

"Why do we need so much money?"

"So that you can get your favourite chocolates, ice-cream, cakes and sweets."

"Oh, but I'm not hungry now, Mummy! So can we play together instead?"

Recognize your child's needs; respect your child's desires and wishes!

Mrs. Mehta was a strict disciplinarian, and always insisted that her children should obey her implicitly. But her youngest son, Jeetu, was difficult.

One day, when the children were out on a picnic and running around happily, she ordered them all to come and sit down on the rug she had spread out.

Reluctantly, the children trooped in to sit down, as they were told. As usual, Jeetu would not heed her call.

Annoyed that he would not obey her, she forcefully carried him and put him down on the rug. "Do as you are told Jeetu ," she said sternly.

Little Jeetu stared sullenly at her. He said nothing for some time, and then, said clearly, "I'm only sitting on the outside; but I'm still running and playing about inside!"

It's not enough to be *teaching* parents; you must also be caring, loving, *understanding* parents!

EVERY CHILD IS A UNIQUE INDIVIDUAL

It was a wise man who said, "Do not try to mould your son in your own image; give him wings, so he can fly and discover his own identity."

In their early years, children are totally dependent on their parents, especially the mother. Caring, loving fathers do help with child-rearing nowadays, but at first, their role can only be to assist the mother.

As babies grow into tiny tots, they continue to depend on their parents for physical, emotional and material support. Fathers are often seen to be carrying older children, while the mother carries the baby.

How often have we not seen children being readied for Pre-Primary School? The mother combs the child's hair, while the father ties his shoe laces; the mother coaxes him to drink his morning glass of milk, as the father prepares to drop him at school.

Parents are so used to the idea that they need to care for their children and protect them, that they sometimes fail to realize that even children have minds of their own and need to be allowed 'to follow their own rainbow', as the saying goes.

Mothers sometimes fume and fret because little girls don't wish to sing and dance and laugh and play.

Priya loved books, even before she could begin to read. Wide-eyed with wonder, she would gaze at the shining covers and the crisp white pages of books with fascination.

When she learnt her A-B-C, there was no stopping Priya's love affair with books. She devoured every book that her caring teachers put before her. At eight years old, she was the school Librarian's favourite; children's encyclopedias and Tell-Me-Why books with questions and answers were liberally lent out to her, for the experienced lady recognized a fellow book-lover in the little girl.

"Bookworm!" scolded her mother, every time she saw Priya curled up in her armchair with a book. "Why don't you take dancing lessons? Why don't you play badminton?"

Priya was the class Topper – continuously. She was a friendly, intelligent, helpful girl, adored by her friends and loved by her teachers. But her mother was sorely disappointed; why didn't she ever come on stage to act in the class drama? Why didn't she participate in the sports events?

At eleven, when Priya went into class six, she was declared to be the outstanding student of the primary school. The school authorities gave the child a scholarship to continue studies in their school.

It was a neighbour who heard the news from her daughter, and told Priya's mother.

"Why didn't you tell me?" her mother asked Priya. "Don't I deserve to share your triumph and happiness?"

"But Ma, you don't really like me, do you?" Priya said, in a small voice. "I don't sing or dance or play games – and that's what you want me to do. If I stand first in class, if I am given a scholarship, that doesn't really mean much to you, does it?"

Don't thrust your ideas, wishes, hopes and aspirations on your children! If you are a doctor, don't expect your son or daughter to take over your clinic from you. If you are an engineer, don't expect your son to follow in your footsteps. Sometimes, mothers who have had cloistered, restrictive upbringing in their childhood want their daughters to live a life of glamour, fame and public adulation.

A famous film star who had started her career as a child-artist, quit the world of glamour and make-believe to marry an impoverished young man of her choice and build her home and family. In her farewell to the film fraternity, she revealed that she had been forced into acting by her ambitious mother, and had hated her life as a star. "It took away my childhood," she said, with tears in her eyes. "I now feel like a bird that has been set free from a golden cage."

Don't plot out your child's life for him, to the final curve. Respect your child's aspirations and personal preferences. Find out what he likes, what he is good at, and encourage him to excel in what he loves – even if you want something else!

Children are not our possessions to 'invest' as we please, they are not lifeless drawings which we can paint or colour as we choose. They are like sensitive plants which must be watered, nourished and protected, so that they may grow and bloom.

Remember the saying, *comparisons are odious*. Don't compare your child with their friends, cousins or neighbours. Don't tell them, "Why can't you dress like Hema?" or "Why don't you behave like Suresh?" or even, "Why can't you be like your brother?"

Every child is a unique individual; if you thrust him into the mould of your making, he will turn out to be the proverbial square peg in a round hole.

Comparison and criticism are not conducive to a child's wholesome development. Instead, develop the spirit of understanding and appreciation. Get to know your child's strengths and weaknesses; realize his limitations; appreciate his talents and unique gifts; encourage him to realize his full potential.

Talk to your child; get to know him well; understand his dreams, fears and aspirations. Consult him about his plans for the future. Allow him to grow and evolve in accordance with his own spirit!

When I was young, the life story of Helen Keller was a source of great inspiration to my generation. Blind, deaf and mute, Helen was lucky to come under the tutelage of a caring teacher, who was determined to do her best for the child. Instead of relegating her to the life of a 'handicapped' girl, her teacher strained every nerve to teach her child to read, write and speak – and grow into a heroic woman who was an exemplary role model for the world to look upto!

Sadly, many children are born with such disorders, and it is up to their parents to ensure that there is no 'handicap' in their growth. I appreciate the positive way we refer to them now – as *differently-abled* children with special needs. If you are parents of such a special child, remember, God has entrusted them to your care, because He believes that you are special parents!

A young couple had had their first child – and their baby boy was born terribly deformed, with just stumps for his arms and legs. The grandparents went into a vortex of grief, cursing and moaning their fate. The young mother's parents even implored the doctor to allow the child to die so that their daughter might not be 'burdened' for a lifetime.

As for the young couple, their grief overflowed as love and compassion. "Our son will need all our help and care," they said to each other. "Thank God, we can offer him all the support he needs."

All parents are not put to such a severe test. But many of them fail to realize the special needs of their 'normal' children.

Many parents in the West are obsessed about their child's IQ. If the child gets only average scores in the school's IQ test, they despair that he is not 'brilliant'.

Dr. E.Paul Torrance, one of America's authorities of intelligence tells us: "IQ tests do not measure creativity. By depending solely on them we miss 70% of our most creative youngsters."

Encourage your child to be curious; to ask questions; to indulge in imaginative visions. Don't be hard on creative children who may not always top the class. Don't moan, "Why can't my son be like other children?" Above all, don't restrain him, hold him back, or clip his wings.

"I don't want my child to be a genius," some people say. "I only want him to be a normal, happy, well adjusted child."

Who is to decide what exactly *normal, happy* and *well adjusted* mean? You? The neighbours?

Dr. Torrance points out that happiness and sound mental health arise out of realizing one's fullest potential.

"Creative people are, in the final analysis, happy people," he says, "provided they are free to create."

Psychologists tell us that today's children are born with much higher IQs than their parents. They are also far more complex beings, born into a world that is becoming more and more complicated. We need to understand them, and respect their special needs. We need to understand their "temperament" and adopt our parenting style to their needs, instead of simply treating them as we think fit.

'Temperament' has been defined as the innate behaviour style of an individual, which seems to be biologically determined. I say *seems to be*, because even advanced research has not come up with definite answers to our questions upon this issue. Knowing the temperament of your child and treating him with understanding can make all the difference – he will grow up to be a happy, not a troubled child; and you will have the satisfaction of evolving into an understanding, appreciating, accepting parent and not a bitter, frustrated parent!

When you understand a 'difficult' child, you can cope with him better – and you can also help him understand himself. Don't react to his behaviour with anger or frustration – rather, accept his nature and then find a strategy to help him adapt in a way that is socially acceptable. This is the 'adult' and 'natural' way to deal with difficult children. And remember, even the most difficult temperamental qualities can work to a child's advantage, when we manage the child sensibly.

One of the most important duties of a loving parent is to help the child grow with a sense of his own self-worth and self-esteem. This does not mean giving in to his tantrums and pandering to his every whim; rather it is helping him to develop a positive notion of himself and giving him a fair idea of his own strengths and weaknesses.

Do Not Discriminate Between Children

Most parents would deny that they have favourites among their own children – although phrases like "Daddy's girl" and "Mamma's boy" indicate the contrary.

It is said that mother's tend to dote on their first born. While the youngest in the family tends to be somewhat neglected, either because the parents are getting older, or because the older children tend to rule the roost.

I myself don't believe in such vague generalizations. However, I do know that in many families, girls are discriminated against boys. Whether it is making finances available for higher/professional education, or allowing mobility and freedom of movement, or even in permitting children to go out with their friends – parents use a different yardstick for boys and girls.

Nina and Naresh are siblings. Though Nina obtained admission to an Engineering College, her parents refused permission to put her in a hostel. "There is no question of allowing a girl to leave home at her age," they said. "Our family would never permit such a thing." And so Nina had to drop her engineering dreams and settle for a Biotechnology course at a local college. Though she is doing very well at her course, Nina is troubled and embittered. Postgraduate courses in her subject are not available in her city. She knows she will come up against the same objections when she completes her degree.

Naresh, on the other hand, was coaxed and cajoled to take up engineering, although he was very poor at Physics and Maths. His parents paid hefty capitation fees to get him admission in a rural engineering college, besides forking out a considerable sum for his hostel expenses. After six years, Naresh has still not completed his four year degree, and is struggling to clear his backlog of examinations. His parents know that he is not likely to get a well paid job after such a poor academic performance. His father plans to mortgage the family owned lands to set him up in an independent business.

Why this discrimination?

Parents of sons have ready answers to such questions. "Who will give his daughter in marriage to my son without an engineering or medical degree? We have our prestige and family name to keep up!"

Does not the 'prestige' and 'family name' extend to educating the daughter equally well?

Apparently not!

A highly educated, intelligent woman confessed to a friend that she still felt hurt about the discriminating references her parents made about her. The phrase *paraaya dhan* (another's wealth) always irked her. "I am *your* daughter, *your* flesh and blood," she would argue with her conservative father. "How could you call me by that name?"

When her father discussed her future, he would often tell his wife, "When Pinky is married off, I will feel really relieved, as if a big burden has been lifted from my shoulders." Pinky would smart at the reference; wasn't she a thinking, intelligent, sensitive human being? Didn't her parents love and cherish her? How then could they think of her as a 'burden' to be cast off, dumped, at the earliest opportunity?

I am sure Pinky's parents had their own justifications to offer – it is an enormous responsibility for the parents to give away their daughter in marriage and to find a suitable boy who would love her and care for her. This is what is referred to as the 'burden' – not the daughter herself.

I doubt whether young ladies today will be happy with that explanation. In India, gender based discrimination, sadly, starts from the womb – so I am told.

Advanced medical technology is used to determine the sex of the foetus in the womb, and I shudder to state this – in some areas, female foetuses are aborted, because a daughter means expense – while a son means income.

I have no hesitation in condemning this as a barbaric practise unworthy of the land that gave birth to Sita, Mira, Gargi and Anasuya. Though the Government has banned these tests, they continue to flourish surreptitiously, illegally, all over the country.

People who will kill the foetus in the womb because it is a daughter, do not deserve to be parents at all!

Recently, a friend told me that a neighbour's daughter had given birth to her first baby. He went to visit the proud grandparents and found the family in the doldrums.

"What's this?" he demanded. "Where is the *mithai*? Where is the happy mother and the lovely child? Why are you so dull and forlorn?"

"*Aree yaar*, it is a girl! What is there to celebrate?" was the shocking response he got.

A few years later, when this same young woman delivered a son, the grandfather ran from pillar to post, to organise a grand party for 300 guests, to celebrate the birth of his grandson!

Grandparents, parents, do not discriminate against the girl child! She is God's gift of love and affection to you. Haven't you heard of the lines:

My son is a son till I find him a wife
But my daughter is my daughter
To the end of my life.

The son-daughter discrimination is one of the most shocking forms of discrimination between children – but other types of discrimination also exist.

The child who is bright and smart is often held up in comparison with the slower, less-gifted child.

Fair, good-looking children are often doted on, while other children take second place in the parent's affection.

As children grow older, sons and daughters who are rich and well-settled, are preferred over their siblings, who have not made the grade in material terms!

Mothers and fathers fall into the trap of favouritism—singling out one child for special affection, and relegating the others to a subsidiary position. Such discrimination can affect the psychological well-being of a child.

Mr. and Mrs. Sharma had four sons—Ravi, Rajesh, Ram and Raghu. Of the four, Rajesh was the one who was reserved and withdrawn. Unfortunately, he hated school and studies, and barely managed to scrape through college. The other three boys did very well and went on the well-trod route of professional courses—medicine, engineering and law.

At 25, Rajesh applied for emigration to Australia; he was selected because of his computer skills.

There was no looking back for Rajesh. With hard work and determination, he grew from strength to strength and became a successful businessman in the land of his adoption. He married Indira, a young Indian student whom he met in Australia. He visits his family once in five years or so—but only to show them how prosperous and rich he is. In private, he tells his friends, "I am what I am today, *not because* of my parents, but *in spite of* them! They never gave me any encouragement or support. They only criticized me and found fault with everything I did. If I had allowed them to influence me, I would have been a failure. I got away from them as soon as I could—and I prospered!"

Rajesh's wife Indira feels that her husband still bears terrible scars of discrimination in his psyche, because of his parents attitude to him.

Actually, Rajesh's parents may not have intended to hurt him. They may have felt that it was necessary to urge him on, to spur him to do better. Little could they have imagined that their treatment could have alienated their son to such an extent!

The scars of childhood and teenage do not heal when children grow into adults. Therefore, treat your children with love and affection in their formative years!

Some parents feel that a little discrimination is justified in the case of gifted children.

When Lalita was seven years old, her dance teacher said to her mother, Mrs. Das, that Lalita would be a great dancer one day. The child's movements, her sense of rhythm and her facial expressions were of the highest order; her talent had to be nurtured carefully.

Mrs. Das was determined that Lalita would get all the support and encouragement she needed. She had to be taken to her regular dancing classes; she had to be taken to watch dance performances and classical ballet; she had to be given a special diet and special facilities for practice at home.

As for the younger child, Leela, she was told, "Be a good girl and take care of yourself. *Didi* needs me."

And so Leela grew up, fending for herself; she learned to comb her own hair; she learned to pack her own lunch; she did her homework on her own;

she read story books in bed and fell asleep on her own—while her mother attended to 'Didi'.

Lalita did fulfill her teacher's promise; she grew up to be an outstanding performer, an artiste par excellence; her entire being was focused on her art and creativity; her mother took care of everything else in her life. Together, they travelled to many corners of the globe; Lalita's performance was applauded and appreciated at cultural festivals in Mongolia and Morocco, Germany and Greece, New Zealand and the Netherlands.

As for Leela, she took care of herself and her father and the home, in her mother's absence. As Lalita had no plans of marriage, a bright young man was chosen to marry Leela. The couple would settle in Delhi, where his family had business interests.

After a lavish wedding, Leela was given a fond farewell by her parents. "Do come home to us whenever you can," said the mother, with tears in her eyes.

"Come home to you?" said Leela, with a glint in her eyes. "You have only one child—and that is Didi. I never meant anything to you—I know I never will, in the future. I have nothing against Didi— for she is totally devoted to her art, and everything else is secondary. But you—you only thought of Didi. I had no mother when I grew up—I only had a father. That is how I will always think of myself—as a motherless child!"

Don't let the special needs of a gifted child blind you to the everyday needs of an average child!

A child who often falls ill; a child with some handicap or the other; a stubborn child or even a child prone to kicking tantrums—such children have a way of demanding your attention and getting more than their fair share. Every mother knows that there are times when one child needs more attention than others—and most mothers know how to balance their time and attention between children. By all means give a difficult or special child the extra attention he needs — but ensure that this does not hurt the sensitivity of the quiet, undemanding child, whose needs are not so clamourous or obvious.

KEEP YOUR CHILD CLOSE TO YOU!

This suggestion applies especially to children in their early years; and this applies especially to mothers. Keep your child very close to yourself, until he is at least three years of age. He needs your affectionate touch, your constant presence, the warmth and security of your loving protection at this stage.

When babies are born, they are wrapped up in a warm bundle and laid close to the mother—for it is believed that the process of 'bonding' begins even at this early stage.

This 'bonding' is very special—for it involves recognition through the senses, of the mother; awareness of the mother, as the closest, most loving, most important being in the consciousness of the child; and familiarity with the person who is going to play a vital role in the child's growth, and the start of a loving relationship which will mean the most to both child and mother.

This is why I urge all mothers, not to leave their children in the care of *ayahs* or paid servants. However busy you may be, however affluent you may be, do not 'delegate' this precious duty to another! How can anyone else replace you, the mother who has cherished and nourished the child in her womb, and given him/her the precious gift of birth and brought him/her out into this wonderful, bright world? How can anyone else be a substitute for *you*? Therefore, keep your child close to yourself; care for him personally, in those crucial formative early years.

I am aware that working mothers these days are under tremendous pressure to resume work soon after the birth of their children. Many of them have to leave their babies in the care of others.

A few of them are lucky to have their parents or parents-in-law, who are only too happy to care for their grandchildren. We in India, can be justifiably proud of this wonderful support system that the family gives us. But as joint families give way to nuclear families, grandparents are not readily available for the care of infants.

Some young mothers are forced to leave their babies in 'crèches'—centers where a lady is paid to care for the baby and give his regular feeds and even nurse him if he is ill. I am told that many employers are also beginning to provide crèches for working women at subsidized charges now — and women find this a boon.

I do not wish to be harsh or unkind—but if young mothers can avoid this, they should try their best to do so! I know that this is a necessary and valuable service offered by women who care about babies and their welfare; I know too, in many cases, young mothers have a very difficult choice before them.

Nevertheless, I urge you — if you can take a break, if you can put your career on the back burner for those two or three crucial, formative years in your child's life, do it! You will find that it is worthwhile!

Many enlightened employers in the West are now beginning to realize the special needs of young mothers, and they offer extended breaks of up to three years, often promising to take them back at the work place, even if it is with a different or lower job description. Others also offer them the opportunity to work from home, till the children are older. These are definitely welcome developments.

On board local flights within India, I am sometimes surprised to see small babies carried by young servant maids, who are practically children themselves! While all the world is demanding that we put an end to 'child labour', here is a strange case of a child paid to carry and look after a younger child!

And, even apart from the ethics or legality of it all, I wonder what sort of mother will find it a strain or a nuisance to carry her child with her on her flight! If it is indeed such a strenuous task, can it be entrusted to a young girl whom you pay to care for the baby?

I think I will never ever find a satisfactory answer to such questions.

Various excuses are brought forward to justify the practice of hiring *ayahs* or baby-minders. "I am not keeping well," "The child is very naughty" or "He is running around all the time and I cannot keep up with him."

Excuses are all very well; but by entrusting the care of the child to paid servants in the formative years, you are taking away the child's right to your personal care and attention, and also depriving him of the comfort and security of your constant presence.

It is said that when God was in the midst of creation, He decided to create woman – who would be the bearer of life in the world. And He said to her:

I hereby endow you with
- *wisdom to recognize truth*
- *courage to deflect all adversity*
- *strength to move mountains*
- *enthusiasm to inspire the world*
- *playfulness, so you can dance with your children*
- *laughter that will echo through the valleys*
- *tears to soothe the sorrows of life*
- *hands that can work or caress*
- *intuition to become what you were meant to be!*

Need I say more about the value of a mother?

When Amanda Sue Greene was born, her father Bob Greene, a journalist with the American Broadcasting Corporation decided to record every detail of her first year. The result was *Good Morning, Merry Sunshine* – a beguiling, unforgettable diary of bewilderment, love, wonder and joy.

"What's the big deal?" some of you might ask. "Dozens of children are born every millisecond, all over the globe. What is this book going to tell us that we don't know already?" Let me reply, using Bob Greene's own words: "I'm sure this has all been happening precisely in this way for uncounted centuries," he writes. "But nobody ever told me!"

Yes — it's happened millions of times and it will happen millions of times again. But when it is happening to your child and you are a part of it — it's wonderful! Why would you want to miss out on this marvelous, magical experience?

The first sight of your child, her first smile, her gradual weight gain, her dawning ability to recognize you and respond to you, her first attempt to turn over, to sit up, to walk, to say da-da or ma-ma—who would want to miss out on these memorable moments meant exclusively for them?

As the child's father, a man should realize that his wife's responsibility is a major one—and that it is his duty to help and support her in every way possible. He should appreciate the young mother's difficulties and readily share the joyous burden of child-care so that she gets relief and rest, and he learns the delicate intricacies of bringing up children.

All child psychologists agree that the first two or three years of a child's life are crucial in his healthy growth and development. A close and affectionate bonding between parents and children during these early years is essential to this vital process.

No one says this is easy!

Just look at the reality: this is recorded by a young mother:

- During the first three months, babies seem to cry constantly—sometimes, for no apparent reason. While this wearies the child, it may exasperate the mother, and drive her frantic with worry.
- Also, during this stage, babies make a mess of their

clothes.

- As they get a little older, they begin to put everything they lay their hands on, right into their mouths.
- They tend to laugh and play and want attention at night—and sleep the day off.
- When they don't get your attention, they turn peevish and angry.
- They have no idea that you may be tired—even exhausted. Babies are utterly self-centred—they cannot help it!

Remember too—that children are like sponges; they absorb things very fast. It goes without saying that children exposed to a particular culture or a particular language in their early years, will naturally adopt it. But this holds true of the parents' lifestyle and interests too! Quarrelsome parents, parents with compulsive eating disorders, couch-potatoes who are watching TV all the time—cannot expect their children to grow up to be healthy, well-balanced and active!

Children of all ages crave time with their parents. It makes them feel special; it makes them feel wanted and secure. This is why parents must create the time to play with their children, on a regular basis. This builds a strong and happy bonding between parents and children. It makes children feel cherished and appreciated—and it also helps parents to discover the uniqueness of the child and understand his mind. And this part of child-rearing is great fun, too! It can be one of the greatest stress-busters even for tired and over-worked parents.

TRAIN YOUR CHILDREN TO PARTICIPATE IN ALL HOUSEHOLD ACTIVITIES

As children, we are always at the receiving end—*taking*, rather than giving. One of the essential characteristics of the mature adult is that we learn to *give*—give of ourselves, our love, our time, our effort and our help.

A child enjoys revelling in the undivided attention and love that his parents lavish on him. As I have said, a child is self-centred; and as long as this attitude persists, children cannot mature into healthy adults.

Erich Fromm puts it this way: The child's maxim is, "I love because I am loved." In other words, the child responds to you only because he knows you love him. The adult maxim is, or should be: "I am loved because I love."

This transition from self-centred child to the caring, giving, sharing, less selfish adult, must begin at home. This is why children must be involved in household chores and activities from an early age.

I am not asking you to dump your responsibilities on the child. When I travel in rural India, I am often saddened to see little girls carrying two of their younger siblings, leading another, holding on to their skirt — obviously playing the role of a surrogate mother, while their poor, over-burdened mother is toiling in a field or a factory.

In Western countries too, older siblings are given the responsibility of baby-minding and looking after the little ones, while their parents are partying or socializing.

What I urge is that children should be trained to participate in all routine household activities like cleaning, dusting, wiping, washing, etc. This will instill in them the spirit of helpfulness and also a sense of respect for manual work. Young boys especially, will learn that it is not their prerogative to be served and waited on.

Mrs. Gupta had two sons — Aman and Arun. Aman, the first, was spoilt like many first-born children. He took his mother for granted; he expected his favourite dishes to be served everytime he sat down to a meal. He left his room in a mess; his clothes were thrown about all over the floor. When he returned home from school/college, he expected to find his room spick-and-span. He expected his wardrobe to be stacked with washed, ironed, fresh clothes which he would use carelessly, dumping them back on the floor. He yelled for coffee, tea or snacks when he needed them—and got what he wanted.

Arun, even as a child, had been called upon to help his mother. He grew up to be caring and sensitive.

He was always ready to run errands for his father — or to help his mother in the kitchen. Chopping vegetables, running the mixer, making tea, toasting bread—nothing was too difficult for him.

The boys were married, and the mother grew to love her daughters-in-law. Aman's wife said to her one day, "Ma, you know you have made life very difficult for me by spoiling Aman. He simply refuses to help me in any way. I wish you had taught him to be a little less selfish."

The mother was taken aback. It had never occurred to her to look at her precious son in that light.

Next time, she asked Arun's wife what she thought of her husband. Pat came the reply: "Ma, you have brought him up to be a wonderful person! I'm lucky to have such an understanding, caring husband—and it's all thanks to you!"

Children must also be taught to do things as well as they can. Eating at table with the rest of the family; packing their school bags; playing with their toys and then putting them away—if they are taught the value of perfection in all they do, they will grow up to be neat, tidy, orderly and disciplined in all that they do.

Geeta has twins who are energetic, naughty and lively. Often this translates into mess and disorder in their room. When the boys started school, Geeta announced a weekly 'reward' for the best-made bed, the neatest half of the room , and the most tidy table. In no time at all, a healthy spirit of rivalry grew among the children, to put everything in place and to keep their room neat and tidy. The children had learnt the value of order and cleanliness!

Taking care of their room and possessions will teach the children to respect the value of everything they are given. They will learn not to damage or break their toys carelessly. They will learn to handle their books, shoes, clothes and toys with care, and not misuse them.

It is said that Sri Sarada Ma, the divine consort of Sri Ramakrishna, once told a young devotee not to handle a broom carelessly—for it, too, had a life of its own.

Such is the sense of respect and veneration that we must instil into our children.

A foreigner who was visiting India for the first time was amazed to see children reflexively doing a 'namaskar' to books or papers which they had accidentally trampled upon. "What a wonderful and noble gesture!" he remarked aloud to his guide. Children take to such precepts very quickly, and grow in the spirit of reverence to everything around them.

Cleanliness, we all know, is next to godliness. Children should be taught to keep their living and playing environment clean.

Don't say, "We have servants to attend to all that!" I know many of you dream of sending your darling sons abroad to USA, UK and Australia for higher studies and better-paid jobs. In Western countries, there are no servants to do our scavenging. Household help is expensive; and the people who offer it are respected and treated well.

I am told that there is a 100-year old law in Germany, which is violated when children refuse to help their parents with household chores like washing up and mowing the lawn. Over a century ago, a wise judge had ruled thus: "Legally, if a child refuses to help his parents, they can go to the court dealing with guardianship matters and have the 'rebel' ordered to work."

The judge also recommended that the following tasks can be 'reasonably' expected from children:

Upto six years old: Nothing but play.

Age six to ten: Occasional help with dish-washing, drying, cleaning and shopping.

Age ten to fourteen: Help with lawn-mowing, full scale dish-washing and cleaning shoes (including parents' shoes)

Age fourteen to sixteen: Car washing and heavier garden work.

Age sixteen to eighteen : Weekly house-cleaning, if both parents are working.

Cleaning the house, helping parents with whatever they do should become second nature to children. We can also inculcate a sense of beauty and order in them, by encouraging them to tidy things up and arrange their books and toys in order.

Children should be taught that all work, all tasks constitute worship of God. When things are done to perfection in the spirit of worship, no task will be thought of as too menial or low. Whether you teach them to arrange flowers in a vase or teach them to clean the bathroom, they should do it with the same degree of attention and care.

As children grow older, you can entrust them with more challenging tasks like carpentry, shelving, mechanical repairs, knitting, embroidery and the use of computers.

If children should happen to spill or break things in the course of such activities, do not be harsh on them. But do not allow them to get injured or work unsupervised. By teaching them to participate in such domestic chores, you train them to integrate hand, heart and head. They acquire the power of concentration and focus; you also awaken their creative instincts and instil a sense of responsibility in them. They will grow up to be independent and self-sufficient; they will also know that helping others is one of the greatest pleasures of life.

Most children grow up and earn their degrees and get into good jobs with comparative ease. What is more difficult is to train them in the art of self-discipline and service. If you want them to master these skills, you have to begin early!

SET GOOD EXAMPLES BEFORE YOUR CHILDREN

Children look up to their elders—especially their parents—to set examples before them. It is not enough to talk about virtues and values, but actually demonstrate them.

Baba Hiren was old and half-blind. He lived with his son Rupen, a busy executive and daughter-in-law Ketki, an active socialite. Baba's wife had died long back. Now, at eighty-two, the light of his life was his grandson, Deepak. The young lad adored his grandfather, who helped him with his homework, played with him when he was lonely, told him stories from the scriptures and epics, put him to sleep every night and helped him get ready for school every morning.

Rupen and Ketki were not bad people—but they had become insensitive to the old man's needs. "My father-in-law lives with us," Ketki would tell her friends in the tone of one who would say, "I deserve an award for patience." Rupen would proudly tell his associates that he had 'given a home' to his father for the last twenty years—as if he deserved a gold medal for the same.

Since his early youth, it had been the custom that the family always had their night meal together. When Rupen had been a little boy, they had sat on the floor of the tiny kitchen with the simple, delicious dishes cooked by his mother placed in the centre, and the three of them facing each other, laughing, joking, coaxing one another to eat more.

Now, times had changed. Ketki had a huge glass-topped table in her dining room, with elegant French chairs. The four of them still ate together—Ketki and Rupen discussing their social life, Deepak and his grandfather chatting quietly in their corner.

Baba Hiren's hands were now trembling severely with age. Sometimes, when they were having soup, the spoon rattled so severely against the bone-china, that Ketki would frown! Deepak began to hold the soup-bowl in his hand, to help his beloved Baba.

"It's becoming an embarrassment to dine with your father," Ketki said to her husband." You must tell him to eat in his own room. We will have a tray sent in to him at meal-time; he can eat as he likes and we can eat in peace."

"No Ketki, I will not allow it!" said Rupen a little apologetically. "We have always eaten together as a family, and that is the way it will stay."

However, that was not to be. One night, as Baba Hiren lifted a glass of water to drink, the glass slipped from his trembling hands and crashed on to the bone-china plate before him. Gravy and rice and vegetables spilled all over the lace tablecloth and on to the French chairs.

"This is the limit," Ketki hissed, her eyes blazing. "Your father cannot eat at the table anymore!"

"Papa, you should be more careful," Rupen said to his father. Turning to Ketki, he said, "Papa will eat with us—but we will not give him a plate or bowl and spoons. He can have semi-solid food in a wooden bowl, which he can sip a little at a time."

So *roti*, vegetables and rice disappeared from the old man's plate—in fact, the plate disappeared too! The cook prepared a bland gruel for him which was brought to him in a fancy wooden bowl—made in Germany!

The old man grew thin, for lack of nourishment, as Deepak watched over him anxiously. One day, he took a spoonful of gruel from his grandfather's bowl, – and made a face: it was bland and insipid!

The following night at dinner, Deepak brought his notebook of clippings to the table. Every student in his school had to keep a scrapbook, where they were expected to note down important events that happened to them and share these notes with the other boys during the Assembly.

That night, they were having *roomali roti* and *paneer koftas* for dinner. It was Baba's favourite menu, but not offered to him that day. The cook brought his gruel on a carved wooden tray and placed it before the old man.

"Excuse me, Raju *kaka*," said little Deepak, flipping open his note book. "Can you give me the recipe for

Baba's *kanji*? I would like to note it down in my scrapbook."

"Certainly Master Deepak," said the cook, clearing his throat. "You take half a cup of broken rice..."

"That's quite enough Raju," snapped Ketki. "There is no need for you to answer silly questions like that. As for you Deepu, don't be so stupid! Why on earth do you want to write down the recipe for gruel in your scrapbook? Your friends will laugh at you!"

"No mama, they won't!" Deepak said to her solemnly. "In fact the boys in my class asked me to bring the recipe."

"What on earth..." began Rupen, thoroughly mystified.

"And, mama, with your permission, I would like to take Baba's wooden bowl and show it to the boys tomorrow," Deepak continued, unabashed.

"You.... What?" Ketki stammered.

"You see mama and papa, Dinoo's father is 38, and Ravi's father is 40 already. It won't be very long before they are like our Baba. So they wanted the recipe for gruel, and they also wanted to see the wooden bowl for themselves. You are 39, aren't you Papa? But I already know how to feed you when you are Baba's age."

There was a clangour as heavy silver spoons fell on bone-china plates and the *paneer koftas* spilled on to the French dining chairs. But this time, the culprits were Rupen and Ketki, who stared at each other in horror.

Rupen was the first to recover. He walked up to his father's chair and removed the wooden bowl of gruel placed before him. "Please take this away Raju," he said to the cook softly. "Bring hot *rotis* for Baba, and the rest of the dishes."

The old man stared at his son, who now put his arms around him; both of them looked at each other through tear-filled eyes. "Forgive me, papa," said Rupen, contrite. "I have been a thoughtless idiot."

Deepak closed his scrapbook with a smile. "I will have to tell the boys that gruel must be cancelled," he announced theatrically. "It seems everyone must have the same food, isn't that so, mama?"

Ketki hung her head in shame.

Inculcate The Spirit Of Unselfishness In Your Child

I would like to begin this section by sharing with you a precious anecdote – a real-life incident from the life of Sadhu Vaswani.

Even as a child, Sadhu Vaswani was the embodiment of the qualities of compassion, self-sacrifice and humane kindness. While his father, Diwan Lilaram, was a man of learning, faith and *tapasya*, his mother, Varan Devi, was a devotee of the Lord, on whose lips and heart, the Holy Name was constantly present. Brought up under her loving care, it was little wonder that Sadhu Vaswani imbibed her piety and devotion.

But even she was surprised by his actions and attitude at times – for he was so different from other children of his age. As he grew up, he grew too, in the qualities of compassion and selflessness.

Sometimes, as he sat down to his meals and heard the cry of a passing beggar, he would take his food and share it with the hungry one.

Often, his mother would find him awake in the middle of a cold, wintry night.

"What's keeping you awake, my child?" she would enquire solicitously of him. "Are you feeling cold? Shall I wrap one more blanket around you?"

She would be startled by his reply: "Mother, the cold I feel cannot be overcome by a hundred blankets or quilts!"

"I do not understand you, my child!" She would tell him. "Speak to me in plain words, not riddles."

Mark the child's words. He said to her, "Mother, I am thinking of hundreds of homeless ones who, in this severe cold, are lying on the roadside. *Their* cold seems to pierce my frame."

From his early childhood, he was filled with the spirit of compassion for all who were in suffering and pain. He had this sense of identification with the poor and destitute, which marked him distinctly, throughout his life. Little wonder, that when he was asked to encapsulate his teaching in a few words, he said simply, "If I had a million tongues, with everyone of those million tongues, I would still utter the one word: Give, give, give!"

This spirit of *giving* should be inculcated in our children from their earliest days. If we teach them to love others, to care and share, to give to those less fortunate than themselves, we will surely sow the seeds of compassion and selflessness in their receptive hearts, and they will grow to be young men and women of character!

Mr. and Mrs. Bhat had managed to secure admission for their daughter in one of the city's topmost, elite schools. As they stood in the long line to pay the hefty admission fees, special fees, caution deposit and sundry other deposits at the school cash counter, they made friends with Mr. Joshi, another parent, whose son was in the fifth standard in the same school. They began to ask him about the school, and what would be expected of them as parents.

"I'll tell you very briefly how best to prepare yourself," said Mr. Joshi, in a matter-of-fact tone. "My advice to you would be to open two hefty bank deposits – one to pay all the special fees, and the other, to pay for all the birthday parties – your own kid's party – and dozens of others to which he will be invited. The children studying here are known to give the most lavish birthday parties – and you will go broke just buying birthday presents, if you do not budget for it !"

Birthday parties for children are growing more and more lavish by the day. My friends tell me that in cities like Delhi, 'Event Managers' have taken on the planning and executing these elaborate affairs. There are 'theme' parties featuring Disney characters or fairy-tale characters; there are 'fantasy' parties depending on the children's preferences. Of course, there is a lavish spread of food and special return gifts for the little guests to take away.

The bill, naturally, runs into thousands!

Don't think I am against children celebrating their birthdays. Your child is God's gift to you, as parents; and I do understand that in your great love for him, you would like to make every birthday memorable for him.

All I ask of you is to teach the child to *give* as well as take, on such occasions. Those of you who have a lavish birthday-budget, spend at least a fraction of the money on disadvantaged children. No, I'm not asking you to send a cheque to some institution; take your child to visit an orphanage or a workers' crèche – and hold a little party there! Let your child share a few goodies with his 'friends' there; let him learn to savour the joy of sharing with his less fortunate brothers and sisters! Believe me, this will transform him and teach him the virtue of selfless giving!

I have no doubt in my mind whatever, that parents today are utterly devoted to their children, and are ready to do everything in their power to make their children happy. Unfortunately, many of them are under the impression that the best way to do this is to lavish expensive clothes, gifts and toys upon them, and provide them with the kind of pocket money that can feed a poor family for a week!

If God, in His grace, has blessed you with such affluence, teach your children to share whatever they have with their less fortunate brothers and sisters! If you are *not* so very affluent, still teach your child to care for others, to give whatever he can.

We live in an increasingly competitive world, where the materialistic, acquisitive urge overwhelms all else in us. Selfishness comes easily and naturally to all of us; it is the other, more difficult spirit of selflessness which must be cultivated painstakingly.

Eight-year old Dimple was out with her father on the beach. A balloon vendor came along with beautiful heart-shaped balloons, silver and red in colour.

"Papa, papa, can I have a balloon?" begged Dimple. At a little distance from there, a bunch of slum-children were watching eagerly – the *sight* of the balloons was excitement enough for them; there was no question of *buying* them.

Dimple's father was not a rich man; but the sight of the eager children and his daughter's pleas worked on his heart. He had kept aside fifty rupees to give Dimple a little treat at one of the food stalls on the beach. On the spur of the moment he gave the fifty rupee note to the balloon vendor and told him to give a balloon each to all the kids standing around.

Ten excited kids were laughing and running around and yelling with glee — Dimple, the happiest among the lot. All she wanted was one balloon – her father had given her ten new friends and a whole load of fun!

There are some children who, when they open their lunch box or unwrap a box of chocolate or a pack of biscuits, will offer it to those around them first, before they themselves take anything.

Is your child such a one? Then you are truly blessed!

Let your children grow in the spirit of unselfishness. Train them to share their food with the starving ones. In ancient times, we are told, no householder would ever sit down to eat with his family, until a poor one had been offered *biksha*. Father, mother, children would stand at the door, ready to offer food, money or grains to passing ascetics and mendicants – and no beggar would be turned away empty handed, from any household!

Does not Sri Krishna tell us in the Gita, "He who cooks for himself alone, is a thief!"

Translate this beautiful message into deeds of daily life for your children. Before they begin to eat their food, teach them to set apart a share for a hungry one – a man, a bird or even an animal; for birds and animals too, are our younger brothers in the One family of Creation.

Teach your children to share and care; to love, give and serve. In this as in all other worthwhile activities, example is always a better teacher than words!

Rich businessmen are often very particular that their children should grow in the awareness that they are very special, very well off, and belong to the exclusive upper strata of society. There is talk of *"Khandaan"*, of family prestige and of habits and activities that suit an upper class lifestyle.

My personal opinion is that children don't have to be taught how to spend money on themselves. It is far more important to teach them how to be thrifty; how to put their wealth to a more compassionate, selfless use; how to share whatever they have with others.

I would therefore urge affluent parents to avoid unnecessary extravagance, pomp and opulence. Instead, children should be taught the value of self-sacrifice.

When Lal Bahadur Shastri was the Prime Minister of India, the nation faced an acute crisis due to an unprovoked aggression from a neighbouring country. In those days, India was not the emerging economic power that she is today. We were a poor country and we had to face a huge deficit caused by our increased defence budget.

Lal Bahadur Shastri was not only a politician of integrity and a statesman with vision; he was also a Gandhian, a man of sterling character. He appealed to the nation – to families, to business establishments, to workers and farmers – to abstain from *one* meal, every week; he chose Monday night as the common occasion for the whole nation, to go on a collective fast, as it were – so that the savings from that missed meal could go towards what was then called our National Defence Fund.

Hotels, restaurants, canteens and snack bars closed down by 6:00 p.m. on Monday. Even Railway Refreshment Rooms did not serve or sell any food. Millions of homes saw no cooking at all on Monday nights – grandparents, mothers and fathers, young men and women, students and little boys and girls, were proud to contribute to a national cause by personal sacrifice!

Encourage your children to give up luxuries and extravagances occasionally. Let them know what it is to fast, what it is to give up a meal every now and then. If you could teach them to go without salt or sugar for a couple of days, they would learn the virtue of self-denial! Let them know what it is like to walk, to take a bus, to be without TV or air-conditioning, to have a simple meal. This will teach them to become aware of how the less privileged live. This will inculcate sympathy and compassion in them, and teach them to extend their love and generosity to the poor and needy.

Thomas Carlyle, the distinguished Victorian writer, was just six years old, when a beggar, wrinkled with old age, knocked at his door.

Little Thomas was profoundly moved by the sight of the old man – his tattered clothes, his bent back and his trembling hands. "Please wait," he said to the stranger, before he rushed up to his room.

He was back in a minute, breathless. In his hand, he carried his precious piggy bank into which he had safely put away the precious pennies and shillings given to him from time to time. Without uttering a word, he emptied the contents of the piggy bank into the grateful hands of the old man.

The little boy was rewarded by the sight of joy-lit eyes and a beautiful toothless smile from the old man.

Recounting this incident, Carlyle said later, "I cannot recall anything that gave me so much pleasure as this simple act of selfless service!"

I know exactly what he meant; for God blessed me too, with such a wonderful opportunity, when I was a child.

This happened when I was about eight years old. Everyday, on my way to school and back, I passed by a toy shop. One of the toys in the shop window was a train-set, which caught my fancy. Every morning and evening, I looked at it with great longing. How I wished I could possess it! What fun I would have playing with it!

One day, I ventured into the shop. I made so bold as to enquire its price. I was told that it cost fourteen annas.

Fourteen annas! It was enough to make me give up all hope of ever possessing the train. Fourteen annas was a pricely sum in those days! We were lucky to get one anna on special occasions.

Every now and then, I would continue to enquire the price of the train set – I was hoping against hope, that it would somehow be reduced, miraculously!

On my next birthday, a miracle came to pass! I was given a one-rupee coin to spend as I liked! I clutched the silver coin tightly in my hand and ran to the toy shop. I would now be able to buy my train!

Just outside the shop, I saw a beggar-woman. She was carrying a sick child in her arms. With tears in her eyes, she called out to everyone who passed by, "Give me alms! My little one has typhoid – and the doctor demands one rupee for the medicine."

How can I describe to you the emotions I felt on hearing that piteous plea for help? Something within me melted; it is also true that I felt a lump in my throat, because I knew I could never ever buy that train again. With one eye, I could see my beloved train in the shop-window; but I could not shut out the sight of the woman with her ailing child.

Wordlessly, I put my precious coin into her outstretched palm. The look in her eyes was my birthday gift – for it taught me what it was to be selfless!

LET YOUR CHILD LEARN FROM NATURE!

Our ancient scriptures tell us that God dwells in all forms and all creatures. In the memorable words of the poet, William Blake:

> To see a world in a grain of sand
> And heaven in a wild flower,
> Hold infinity in the palm of your hand
> And eternity in an hour...

Does this not reflect the belief of the Hindus, that the One spirit infuses all Creation – that all that is, is a vesture of the Lord?

It is essential that children must be made to realize this great truth – that God dwells in every aspect of His creation; and therefore they must be taught to respect and revere all aspects of Nature, including birds, animals, fish and insects; trees and plants and shrubs; even rocks and stones and sand.

Sadhu Vaswani taught us that flowers have their 'families', even as we do! Therefore, to this day, we avoid plucking flowers for any form of worship or devotion at the Mission campus.

Does not the Holy Quran tell us:

There is no beast on earth, no bird which flieth but…the same is a people like unto you. All God's creatures are God's family.

Teach your children to revere nature: for, in the words of the *Ishopanishad*:

Of a certainty, the man who can see all creatures in himself, himself in all creatures, knows no sorrow.

Parents must take the trouble to inculcate in the children love and reverence for nature from an early age. Encourage them to plant seeds and saplings in your garden, balcony or even a window box. Let them watch nature at work, as the seed miraculously sprouts, grows and blooms into flower and leaf. Let them watch the magic of nature before their eyes, under their own little hands!

Teach them to wake at dawn and behold the beauty of the rising sun; teach them to appreciate the myriad hues of twilight and sunset; teach them too, to marvel at the millions of twinkling stars and the silver moon at night.

The great Romantic Poet, William Wordsworth, was a profound believer in the healthy, soothing, enlightening, moral influence of nature, especially on growing children. To Wordsworth, nothing in nature was trivial or ordinary: daisies, larks, cuckoos, or even the green grass underfoot. Deeply sensitive to the spiritual as well as physical influence of nature, he believed that Nature had the power to teach moral truths and to influence one's character:

One impulse from the vernal wood
Can teach us more of man
Of moral evil and of good
Than all the sages can.

Our children cannot all grow up to be nature poets. But surely, they can be taught to draw inspiration and delight from nature. For nature has a way of influencing our emotions, of instilling calm, peace and serenity into our souls. Children's emotions, especially, can be tuned to respond favorably to the influence of nature.

The earth is not an inanimate planet – it is imbued with God's life, it is full of the breath of the Infinite Being. The source of natural beauty is none other than God, the loving Father of us all. Thus, a sense of kinship, of communion with Nature, can lead us on to the awareness of the "Universal Benevolence" which rules all the world.

One moment now may give us more
Than years of toiling reason:
Our minds shall drink at every pore
The spirit of the season...

Books are not the only storehouses of wisdom; sermons are not the only source of moral values; the woods, the trees, the mountains, rivers and valleys can teach our children to revere life and value the great gifts that the Creator has bestowed on us.

Let me give you Blake's unforgettable poem, "The Lamb" from his *Songs of Innocence*:

Little lamb, who made Thee?
Dost thou know who made thee,
Gave thee life and bid thee feed
By the stream and over the meed –
Gave thee clothing of delight,
Softest clothing, woolly, bright,
Gave thee such a tender voice,
Making all the vales rejoice?
Little lamb, who made thee,
Dost thou know who made thee?

This is not just a poem to amuse and delight little children. It also teaches them a profound truth: God created us, gave us the great gift of life and bestowed on us several other blessings – like the beautiful world we inhabit; like our precious senses and the intelligence which animates us; our unique attributes and abilities and a million other comforts and delights that we ought to be grateful for. The point is, are we aware of our Creator, of His plans for us, of our obligations to Him?

The sight of a little lamb can teach the children all these, and more valuable truths!

Parents must also inculcate in children the attitude of reverence for nature, and the impulse to protect and conserve nature. The boy who tortures caterpillars and beetles and captures butterflies in glass jars, will grow up to be cruel to his friends in school. Indeed, I cannot emphasize this enough – if children indulge in cruelty to animals, this will have serious repercussions in their later life. And so, when you see your children being cruel to animals or insects, alarm bells should ring within, to remind you that you are failing in your duty to bring them up as caring, compassionate beings!

I urge all parents to take the time and effort to teach their little ones to be kind and compassionate to animals. This attitude of protection to dumb and defenceless creatures is far more valuable than numerical, verbal or computer skills in their early years – for it will make them better human beings!

The Hindu way of life teaches us to revere nature in all its myriad forms. The *Tulsi* is associated with Lakshmi, the *Vilwa* is associated with Lord Shiva; the banyan tree is sacred too; the humble mouse is the vehicle of our beloved Lord Ganesha, who Himself takes the form of the magnificent elephant; Hanuman, the strong, wise and devout servant of Sri Rama, is a *Vanara*, the form of the monkey; and in every Hindu household, *go puja* or devotion to the gentle mild cow, is indeed special!

Allow your children to participate in such forms of worship so that they learn to behold the world of Nature as a part of their existence. Children must be taught that the kindness and compassion they show to all forms of life will do *them* more good than the creatures for whom they do it!

Nature is also a valuable teacher which teaches us to give and serve – silently!

> God made the sun – it gives
> God made the moon – it gives
> God made the stars – they give
> God made the air – it gives

God made the clouds – they give
God made the earth – it gives
God made the trees – they give
God made the flowers – they give
God made the *plan* – He gives
God made man – he…?

I remember the beautiful day we spent in a garden, sitting at the Lotus Feet of Sadhu Vaswani. He pointed to some beautiful flowers and said to us : "Look at these flowers! How beautifully they bloom! But they do it silently. Even so must you serve silently. These flowers spread their fragrance in silence – even so must you serve in silence."

Then, pointing to the sun, he said, "The sun, even as it shines, sends life-giving warmth and light to the earth. But it shines silently! And remember, there are millions, billions, perhaps trillions of trillions of creatures whose very existence depends upon the sun – but the sun shines silently. Even thus must you serve silently!"

Can there be a better teacher for our children than Mother Nature?

Don't be satisfied with taking your children to amusement parks, shopping centres and fun-fairs. Take them into the great outdoors to marvel at the wonderful panorama of Nature; take long walks with them in wide open spaces; let them feel the bracing hush of the cool breeze on their faces; let them breathe in the fresh, clean air of the open countryside; let them learn to love the greenery of the grass, the leaves and the tall trees; let them watch the flow of the rivers and streams; let them discover the mystery of the woods and forests; let them marvel at the lofty roof that is the sky.....

Let them learn too, that compassion to all living creatures is the essence of humane existence. Kindness to dumb and defenceless creatures is our obligation, our responsibility, our sacred duty:

A robin redbreast in a cage
Puts all heaven in a rage,
A dove-house filled with doves and pigeons
Shudders hell through all its regions...
Each outcry of the hunted hare
A fibre from the brain does tear.
A skylark wounded in the wing
A cherubim does cease to sing.

Teach your children too, that nature is a manifestation of God. God comes to us, putting on different vestures, different garments. Clad in different garbs and different forms, the Lord appears before us as a lamb, as a bird, as a flower, as a stone – to find out if we truly love and revere Him. Alas! We slay the Lord! We abuse Him. We handle Him roughly, we treat Him harshly. We offer Him worship in temples and churches; we chant hymns to His glory – but out in the streets we are cruel to Him! We slay Him and eat His flesh!

Much upon this earth is masked. But there is a strange, mystic sense of fellowship with all that lives. Let your children discover this transcendental spirit in the world of Nature!

THE FAMILY THAT PRAYS TOGETHER, STAYS TOGETHER

The home is the door to the Kingdom of God. Therefore, everyday, all the members of the family – from the youngest to the eldest – should spend a little time in prayer together. Let all the members of the family get together, at an appointed time everyday, at a little, exclusive family *satsang* – even if it is for no more than ten to fifteen minutes. I assure you this will give a new tone, a new life, a new spirit to your home!

I urge all my friends to keep at a prominent place in their home, a big beautiful picture of their *ishta devta* or of a great heroic soul – Krishna, Rama, Buddha or Jesus, Zoroaster, Mahavir, Guru Nanak or Baha'u'llah – to whom they feel drawn. Whenever you or the children enter the house or leave it, bow down to the picture and offer a brief mental prayer. You will be amazed at the difference it makes to your day.

Many people tell me that it is not possible for them to take the children to *satsang* everyday. You can have your own *satsang* at home, by creating the right ambience and right atmosphere. Let the lamps be lit; do a little *kirtan*; read a thought from a scripture, or an incident from the life of a great soul; let each and every member offer his or her reflection on what has been read out; at the end, let everyone join in the *aarti*; let the children be given some *prasad*.

From time to time, arrange a service programme in which the children also participate. They will thus learn to pray not only with their lips and hearts but, also, with their hands.

To enhance the faith and piety of the children, it is essential that we narrate to them stories of God, the *avataaras*, of saints and spiritual leaders. This will make them aware of the great power, the divine *shakti* that moves the entire universe.

Encourage your children to turn to God in prayer, for all that they need. Many people are under the impression that it is wrong to ask God to fulfill our material needs. I don't think this is true.

I believe that we have two options; either to ask worldly people, or ask God for what we want. Need I say which is the better option?

I believe too, that children should become aware that God is our Father, Mother and Friend.

Twameva mata cha pita twameva….

Why then should we hesitate in asking for anything from our father or mother? To whom else can a child turn, if not to his mother and father?

All God wants is that we turn to Him – for whatever reason. In the measure in which we think of approaching Him, our level of consciousness rises!

That is the beauty of prayer! Let the children pray for whatever they desire – their consciousness will keep on rising, until one day, they will begin to ask God for His Love and His Mercy – and nothing else besides!

Teach children too, to realize that God answers all our prayers in three ways: 1) To some of our prayers, He says, "Yes, my child! What you ask is good for you, and I will grant it to you." 2) To some other prayers, He says, "No, my child! What you are asking is not the right thing for you. Therefore, I will not grant it to you." 3) His third answer is : "Wait, my child! I will give you what you want – but in good time. The right time has not yet come."

Yes, No and Wait – let the children know that these are the three answers.

Regular, daily prayer at home can play a vital role in shaping the character of your children. Other spiritual practices can include the following:

- Meditation and yoga, taught under the guidance of a special teacher trained to impart them to children
- Repetition of the Name Divine
- Reading the scriptures and the *bani* of great ones.
- Study of great *puranas* like the *Ramayana* and *Mahabharata*
- Practice of *likhit japa* – writing of the Name Divine

Many of my friends who live abroad also request the Sadhu Vaswani Mission to organize special camps, weekend retreats and summer schools for children where they can imbibe the values and ideals of our Hindu culture.

When prayer becomes a part of your child's life, it lays down the spiritual foundation for his wholesome development. When you teach your child to cultivate absolute faith in God, you are also teaching him to tackle all problems – physical, emotional and spiritual – in the best possible way.

Teach your children too, the value and power of silence. Living in this fast, noisy age, children are often full of restless energy. It is vital that you teach them to sit still and observe silence for at least a few moments. Sitting in prayer or at the *satsang* must become an effective way of calming them down, and helping them to overcome their restless nature.

Teach your children to surrender themselves to the grace of God and the Guru. Let them realize that God and the Guru are always at hand to protect them, guard them and prevent them from yielding to evil and temptation. Teach them to remember their God and Guru first thing, when they awaken, and last thing, before they fall asleep. They should be taught also, to repeat the Name of God and their supplication to the Guru, during the course of the day. This will help them do well in their studies, it will give them better concentration and focus; it will guard them from all danger and evil.

There was a man of God who spread the sunshine of faith, hope, joy and optimism wherever he went. Whomsoever he met, he changed their lives for the better.

"What is the secret of this great joy that seems to radiate from your very presence?" they asked him.

In answer, he narrated this incident from his life.

Years earlier, when he decided to leave home to tread the spiritual path, his mother walked along with him to the outskirts of the village, to bid him farewell and to bestow her blessings on his spiritual quest.

Knowing that she would have to say goodbye to her loving son – perhaps never to see him again – she said to him, "Promise me one thing before you leave."

"What is it mother?" he asked her gently.

"Promise me first," she insisted.

"As you wish, dear mother," said the young man, "I promise to do as you wish."

"This is what I wish," said the mother earnestly. "Dear son, it is a wicked world into which you go to seek your salvation. I want you to be safe from all harm and evil. Therefore, promise me this – begin every day with God; and close every day with God. This is all I ask of you." And she kissed him fondly on the forehead.

"It was this kiss – and this promise that my mother asked of me – that gave direction to my life," the holy man concluded. "My mother taught me the true secret of joy and peace – begin the day with God; and end the day with God."

Teach your children too, the secret of joy and peace – make God real in their lives, through the practice of daily prayer!

WHY DO CHILDREN
GO ASTRAY?

Two thousand five hundred years ago, Aristotle, who may be described as the founder of western education, western philosophy and logic, said of teenagers that they were impulsive, prone to excess and exaggeration and lacking in self-control. Therefore, he concluded, young men of his day were unfit to study philosophy.

We might be pardoned for concluding that human nature has not changed all that much in the last two millennia! Down the centuries, the adolescent years, the teenage years have always been troublesome and problematic for parents and children.

There are notable exceptions, let me hasten to add. We hear of highly motivated teenagers, dedicated youngsters who set themselves high targets in academics, sports, technical skills, arts, music and other interests, and make their families proud by their splendid achievements.

On the other side of the divide, there is cause for concern and worry. Common adolescent problems reported the world over are delinquency, drug use, academic failure, sexual deviancy, not to mention emotional disorders like depression, anxiety, rebellion and even proneness to suicide.

Here are some statistics gathered by American researchers:

- During the 1980's in the U.S. adolescents who comprised merely 14.3 % of the population, accounted for over 35.5 % of non-traffic related arrests.
- Between 1986 and 1991, there was a 48 % rise in the number of youths arrested for serious crimes like rape, robbery, assault and homicide. In 1991 alone, 130,000 teenagers were arrested for these offences.
- In the 12-17 age group, one out of four youngsters reported using illicit drugs.
- One-third of all high school seniors reported daily intake of alcohol.
- One out of five high school seniors admitted to regular cigarette-smoking.
- Several teenagers admitted to 'risky' or 'deviant' sexual behaviour – having multiple partners, contracting sexually transmitted disease etc.
- Approximately every minute, an adolescent (unwed) girl gives birth to a baby in the U.S.

My friends, I am not singling out the U.S. as a problematic area. It is just that there are statistics and records available in the U.S. for all these social problems. India, Indonesia, U.K. and Europe must be facing such problems too. While the frequency and magnitude of these problems might vary, it is obvious that youngsters everywhere are caught in such undesirable behaviour patterns. Psychiatrists in fact categorize a ten-year period—between 13 and 23—as a 'dangerous decade' for all youngsters, when such problems escalate, sometimes beyond acceptable limits.

Many adolescent children today are prone to 'get into trouble' one way or another. Parents are shocked and grieved when their children are caught copying in exams, shop-lifting, absenting themselves from school/college, or indulging in drugs/alcohol/cigarettes. When caught in the act, these children are often as confused and upset as their parents—they simply cannot explain why they have behaved so badly. As for the parents, they are anxious, worried and terribly afraid; they blame themselves, or turn against their children in anger; there is a sense of betrayal, frustration and guilt.

Sometimes, even without resorting to excesses, children cause extreme anxiety to their parents by aggressive, defiant and disobedient behaviour. They repeatedly break the rules of the home and indulge in bad behaviour without any sensitivity or concern for the other members of the family. This may include:

- losing one's temper
- persistent and rude arguments with parents
- defying rules and regulations
- blaming parents and siblings for their bad behaviour
- initiating, annoying and provoking family members without any rhyme or reason
- being spiteful, vindictive and emotionally volatile

Consider the following instances:

Thirteen-year old Rita is playing a computer game as her mother repeatedly calls her to join the rest of the family for dinner. For ten minutes, she only says, "Coming!" "Coming!" Finally, her mother enters Rita's room and switches off the computer and orders her to come to the dining table.

Sulking and defiant, Rita reaches the table and dinner starts. (It is the unwritten rule in their family that at night, all the members eat together at the table.)

As the food is served and the younger children are chattering gaily, Rita makes a face at the food on her plate. "Not cabbage again!" she grinds her teeth. "Disgusting! I don't want it."

"Behave yourself Rita," says her mother. "Look at your brother and sister! How well-behaved they are! Shouldn't you set an example before them?"

"You can't have potatoes and *channa* every day," says her father sternly. "Don't complain about the food. And learn to behave pleasantly when we are at the table."

"I hate cabbage, I hate the food in this house and I hate all of you!" screams Rita. "You don't care for me! I'm tired of your endless lectures and I am getting out of this place because I am beginning to suffocate here..."

With that outburst, she walks out of the flat, slamming the front-door behind her. The younger children gasp in shock, the mother dissolves into tears; the father stares at his plate, unable to react...

Fifteen year old Nitin was playing his favourite music in his room. Although the door was shut, the sound of the drums and guitars was deafening.

"Ma, I can't do my home work," complained his twin, Nikita.

Their mother, a school teacher, was assessing examination papers. Annoyed at the excessive noise, she knocked at Nitin's door. Nitin could not hear the knocks, so absorbed was he in the music. After repeated banging and tapping on the door, he finally emerged, still rocking to the music.

"Nitin, turn down the volume of your music system at once," his mother shouted. In fact, she had to yell just to make herself heard in all that din.

"Huh?" said Nitin, pretending he couldn't hear. "What are you saying, lady?"

The flippant answer and the pretended deafness was the last straw for Nitin's mother. Angrily, she strode into the room and turned down the volume. Nitin waited for her to get back to the door and then turned up the volume to an even louder level.

"That's quite enough Nitin," screamed the irate mother. "Don't cross your limits, I warn you!"

As Nitin tried to prevent her from touching his audio system, the mother yanked the plug from the socket and threw it down.

His twin sister giggled at the battle of tempers between her mother and brother.

"How dare you, Mom!" blazed Nitin, stung by his sister's laughter. "How dare you barge into my room and mess about with my equipment? Is this the kind of manners you teach your students at school?"

The sister stopped laughing, her mouth fell open in astonishment. Her mother turned red with mounting anger and impulsively raised her hand as if to slap her misbehaving son.

Nitin caught her hand in a tough, tight grip. "Don't!" he warned her. "If you raise your hand again, you will live to regret it," he said to her through clenched teeth.

"Stop it Nitin!" said the mother, trembling now. "How dare you talk to me like that! Apologize for your bad behaviour this minute!"

"*You* apologize to me first," screamed Nitin. "You barge into my room and spoil my holiday—why should *I* apologize to you? I am fed up of your constant do's and dont's. I can't wait to leave this house and get away. It is just like a prison and you are worse than a jailor!"

With that, Nitin knocked all the books off his table, kicked the shelf which stored all his CDs, banged his guitar against the wall, smashing it right through and stormed out of the room.

His mother stood still, as if she was in a trance; she could not believe this was happening to her. Only a couple of hours earlier, Nitin had demanded that she bake his favourite chocolate cake. The cake was in the oven now. What had come over her son? She had only wanted him to turn the volume down....

Such needlessly aggressive behaviour leaves parents bewildered and anxious. "What's wrong with our child?" they wonder. Or, "What have I done wrong?"

Even worse than temper tantrums are delinquency, violence and criminal behaviour. Some years ago, a bunch of decent well-to-do boys in Pune were caught in the act of stealing motorbikes and scooters. They had made it their hobby to use illicit keys to start expensive two-wheelers parked in the streets and take them on high-speed 'joy-rides' through the city. Sometimes, they would deliberately run the bikes into walls and pavements and damage them; sometimes, they would simply abandon them in a different part of the city. When the gang was caught, it was discovered that these boys went to some of the best schools in the city, and their fathers included lawyers, doctors and senior government officials. What could have prompted these teenagers to indulge in such criminal behaviour?

A quiet, timid, middle-aged woman, dressed in poor, shabby clothes approached the security guard of a well-known girls' college in Bangalore. She wanted to know if the NCC girls had returned from their Camp in Mysore.

The guard was a courteous, kind soul. He led the woman to the College NCC Office and introduced her to the Professor-in-Charge. The woman explained to the Professor that her daughter, Lata, was in the First Year and had left for her week-long camp in Mysore on the previous Tuesday. She was to have returned on Monday. It was Wednesday now and there was no information from the daughter. The poor woman, who rarely ever left her house, had walked all the way to the College, in her anxiety to enquire about her daughter. Could Madame give her any information about Lata....?

The Professor was taken aback. The college had not organized any NCC Camp for its students.

Enquiries at the office revealed that Lata had taken 10 days' leave on the pretext of attending to her mother, who was hospitalized.

Uncomprehending, the woman said, timidly, "But I am fine! Why should I go to hospital?"

The truth dawned on her suddenly. Her daughter had lied to her, bluffed the college authorities and had taken off to some unknown destination... Oh horror of horrors! What would become of her now?

Recently, the Government of India had appointed a Central Commission to go into the question of 'ragging' in colleges. What makes young students turn into monstrous bullies, traumatizing and scandalizing their juniors?

In the news too, were sons of affluent businessmen and prominent politicians caught with drugs in their possessions. At a New Year's Eve Party in a farmhouse near Pune, over 300 youngsters were caught using drugs. What could have prompted them to ruin their future by a criminal record of this sort?

Unfortunately, such cases are becoming more and more frequent and parents of teenagers are becoming increasingly anxious about the moral and emotional well-being of their children.

Psychiatrists say that some of the following conditions may be responsible for problem behaviour :

- Family conflicts
- Poverty / financial difficulties at home
- A tough school curriculum/system with which the child is not able to cope, and faces repeated academic failure

- Undesirable elements in the peer group / friends' circle—such as children who indulge in tobacco / alcohol abuse, and are prone to violence and delinquent behaviour
- History of violence in the family

As we can see, the family plays a major role in influencing children's behaviour; any instability or tension in the family, such as financial loss, illness, divorce and death can contribute to the volatility and aggression of teenage children.

With or without extreme measures like divorce and separation, most families go through some crisis or the other as children grow up. In some cases, it might be a simple factor such as the father being transferred to a distant place, while the mother stays behind with the children, so that their schooling is not affected. In another family, it might be a more serious problem, like one of the parents contracting a major illness, which disrupts the normalcy of family life. In other cases, it might be constant and persistent quarrelling between the parents which affects the children psychologically.

"But Dada, this is the human condition today," some people might argue. "How can any family isolate itself from illness, disease, death and change of fortunes?"

True, there are situations and circumstances we cannot change. But there are positive attitudes and behaviour patterns that we can put into practice to help protect our children from adverse influences.

UNDERSTANDING YOUR TEENAGER

Sometime ago, a distraught couple met me after one of my public lectures in a foreign country.

"Dada, we have gone through a lot as parents, but we have always stuck together and faced problems successfully," the husband said. "But now, I am afraid we are thoroughly demoralized."

"I have nursed my daughter through severe illnesses and coped with her childhood temper tantrums," added the wife. "Now I feel I have failed miserably as a mother. I cannot cope with her any more."

The subject of their 'problem', their 'cause for concern' was standing just a few feet away, chatting to young people of her own age. To all outward appearances, she was a normal, healthy, energetic teenager—an adolescent among a million other adolescents.

Why is it that parents who have brought up their kids successfully till the age of ten or eleven, suddenly find themselves unnerved by the onset of adolescence in the children? What is so problematic about adolescence?

The teen-years, the years of adolescence, the transition period from childhood to adulthood, the *troublesome decade* as some have called it, is actually a period of intense growth—physically, intellectually, emotionally and morally—for the children.

For some children, adolescence comes early—others can be late starters. Some children shoot up in height and weight to become virtual giants, while others take time to grow up. But apart from these visible, physical changes that we are aware of, children are also going through complex inner changes.

Adolescence can be a difficult and challenging time not only for caring parents—but also for their confused children. Teenagers are often overwhelmed by the physical and emotional changes that they are going through. The parents, I would say, are comparatively better off: they only have to worry about their child; but the child is facing pressure from several quarters—from the immediate family circle, from his/her peer group, from teachers and school authorities, and from society at large. Everybody seems to have high expectations about them—they are supposed to look good, dress well, behave perfectly, conform to appearances, excel in studies and if possible, do well in sports and other extra-curricular activities.

As children pass through this difficult transition period from childhood to adulthood, they also begin to feel the first stirrings of a strong desire to be *independent.* This first step towards maturity is in itself positive—but in the teenage years, this impulse is in conflict with the child's obvious *dependence* on the parents in so many aspects of his life. He knows fully well that he needs his parents not only for food, shelter and clothing, but also for his good schooling, his favourite clothes, gadgets, computer and two-wheeler—and above all, he *does* need the security and protection that their love alone can give him

At the same time, he is also trying to assert his own identity, create his own 'image' ! Thus many children begin to experiment with clothes, hairstyles and even with new values and a new way of behaviour and speaking. So we find girls cutting their hair very short, or dyeing their hair in what their parents consider to be 'weird' colours. Boys pierce their ears, even sport 'ponytails'. Shabby jeans and faded shirts are preferred articles of clothing.

All this is, of course, highly embarrassing, even humiliating for their parents. Unfortunately, they begin to criticize the children's behaviour, giving them negative feedback and creating bad feelings.

Many children are also uncomfortable about their bodies—especially their overall shape, height and weight. Some children put on a lot of weight, leading to severe eating disorders. Boys are worried that they are not growing tall enough, while girls are ashamed of their sudden spurt in growth. Either way, the children are unhappy and uncomfortable with the way they look. They have lost the happy, unselfconscious attitude of childhood; and they are still years away from the assured self-confidence of young adulthood; trapped in between, they often develop what we call a 'complex', suffering from low self-esteem. Girls begin to suffer acutely because they are not fair and slim and pretty like some of their friends. Boys are disgusted because they are not tall and strong and smart.

These may seem superficial concerns to us. But they assume serious proportions for our teenagers.

That is not all. Teenagers are subject to diverse pressures which they are not able to cope with—pressures that you and I can take in our stride. Their friends and peers set certain standards for them and raise certain expectations which are in direct conflict with their family values. Friends and peers tempt teenagers to try cigarettes, alcohol and drugs. "Come on, it's all just for fun," they are told. Classmates gang up together to 'cut' school lessons and go off to movies. And if money happens to be short, children are urged to 'borrow' money from father's wallet or mother's handbag—without their knowledge and permission.

Teenagers are also exposed to new conflicting issues such as race, gender, religion and moral values.

"Is it true that you worship monkeys and elephants in India?" asked an American friend, leaving fourteen-year-old Mira confused and ashamed. In her heart of hearts she wished she had been born a Christian, so that she could be just like her American peers.

"Are you really my parents, or did you simply adopt me?" cried fourteen year old Tina, accusing her parents of partiality and injustice. Her brother was allowed to come and go as he pleased and dress as he liked, while all sorts of rigorous restrictions were placed on her dress and movements.

On her fifteenth birthday, Pooja treated all her friends to ice cream at Baskin Robbins. Even as Priya enjoyed her friend's birthday treat, she felt secretly ashamed that she had only distributed toffees to her friends on her own birthday. That evening, when she went home, she threw her school bag on the ground and said rudely to her mother, "How do you expect me to get by on fifty rupees as pocket money? I cut a sorry figure before my friends!"

Very often, teenagers are so confused that they cannot understand or explain their own behaviour. They simply see rude behaviour and aggression as appropriate ways of dealing with the various problems they face.

There is one important fact that parents need to understand: while teenagers crave independence and wish to take charge of their own lives, in their heart of hearts they still need parental guidance, approval and support. This is perhaps the fundamental conflict which they cannot understand, resulting in behaviour problems.

One of the most important things that parents need to teach their teenage children is the ability to take responsibility for their own actions and develop a sense of commitment to themselves and their future.

This is certainly not an easy task that can be executed overnight! Parents, teachers and other elders in the family need to help teenagers to develop their sense of maturity, responsibility and awareness.

It is not that all of us, as adults, have acquired this independence effortlessly. Many of us are still daunted by the sheer necessity of making decisions. We lean on our near and dear ones for support and guidance. In truth, our search for independence does not end when we reach adulthood. At every age, at every stage in life, we are challenged to face new problems, take tough decisions, and acquire more and more self-reliance. If, as adults, we continue to face such problems, what of our confused, immature young teenagers? How tough it must be for them to acquire the ability to think rightly, and make correct moral choices on their own, even while they are susceptible to so many outside influences, and vulnerable to negative inputs!

During their teenage, children begin to be more exposed to people and events outside their immediate family circle. They are making new friends, developing new interests, widening their circle and often have more opportunities to govern their own behaviour —i.e. to behave more or less responsibly, more or less morally, more or less acceptably, more or less in conformity with parental expectations and values.

"Hi Rajesh! How come you're driving a car!" exclaim his friends, as they see Rajesh drive in stylishly in a new Honda City.

"When the cat is away the mice will play," laughs seventeen year old Rajesh. He is not old enough to drive a car; he has not even taken formal driving lessons. But his parents are away to attend a family wedding, and it has been a lark to bully his old grandmother and drive his father's Honda to a friend's party tonight. What an impression he has made, too!

"Wow, Leena, you look like a film star!" chorus her friends as Leena walks into a party with garish clothes and excessive make-up.

"I am enjoying myself, dressing up as I please," giggles Leena, not aware of the grotesque appearance she presents. "My mother is on a foreign tour, and there's no one to tell me what to wear and what not to wear."

Teenagers today are often out of the ambit of direct supervision by their parents. As mothers and fathers try to balance precarious demands of career and home, professional and family life, teenage children have to cope with self-governance and independence.

While many teenagers are apt to imagine that they are acquiring maturity and independence, they are unaware that they are being influenced, even swayed, by peer pressure and the need to impress their friends and gain their approval. Thus while they think they are acting independently, they fail to realize that they are rejecting their parents' ideals only to be governed by the influence of their friends.

Parents want their children to conform to family values and expectations, and many teenagers resent this – and even reject this. "I don't want to be a doctor," asserts a young student angrily. "Just because you and Mom are doctors, doesn't mean that I should be interested in medicine."

"I hate classical music and classical dance," a young girl cries out to her mother. "Why do I have to do what *you* like? I want to take up karate and swimming. Do you mind?"

These children seem to know their own minds, and that is good. But the trouble is, they are unaware that their 'choices' are actually governed by peer-pressure—the interests and influences of their friends.

Reena's friends think modeling is the ideal career to make money and become famous, and Reena is unduly influenced by them. She would rather 'conform' to her friends' expectations, than bow to her parents' wishes and take up Computer Science. Ram's classmates are determined to quit studies as early as possible and take up a lucrative call center job which offers so much easy money and an exciting lifestyle and a new group of friends. Ram therefore thinks that his parents are foolish and old-fashioned to insist that he should take up Engineering.

Neither Reena nor Ram realize that they are rejecting parental influences only to 'conform' to peer pressure. This is hardly true independence! While they stop taking advice and guidance from their parents, they are beginning to rely on friends and peers for the same advice and support. Thus their behaviour, value systems, dress and habits are all in truth, dependant on and determined by peer-pressure, or the highly doubtful role-models they see on TV and cinema. This is certainly not true independence or maturity.

Children need to become truly self-reliant, mature and independent. They must learn to make the right choices and take the right decisions without undue influence by their peers. They must take charge of their lives and learn to interact maturely and positively with people inside and outside the family circle. In order to acquire this maturity and independence, they have to develop a sense of autonomy, with a judicial measure of help and support from their parents.

In the crucial teen years, children are struggling for more independence and very often, parents want to assert more control over their lives. This may lead to family conflicts in some cases—but such conflicts can be avoided if there is closeness and communication between family members.

How Can Parents Help Their Teenagers?

M y first advice to parents in this connection would be: don't blame it all on your teenager!

Family environment and the prevailing tensions in the home play a major role in affecting the behaviour of teenage children. For example, constant quarrels and heated arguments between the parents, persistent airing of grievances and complaints, and hostility between family members can adversely affect the children's behaviour patterns. Therefore, in the words of Carlyle: *Bobus, reform thyself!* Or, to use the modern equivalent, *Physician, heal thyself!* Parents cannot indulge their ill-will and nasty temper as 'adults' and expect their children to be perfect!

Many teachers in schools and colleges will tell you that strains and tensions in the family are often reflected in the mood, behaviour and academic performance of their students. Unable to confront their parents' negative attitude, these children often open up to their friends and teachers, looking for help and support which their parents have failed to give them. An understanding aunt, grandmother or neighbour can also be a source of strength at such times. But this underlines the fact that the parents have failed the child, let the child down, forcing him/her to look elsewhere for support.

Therefore, let not 'parental problems' contribute to your teenager's troubles. In the West, they have Family Counseling and Parenting support groups to help couples overcome such problems. In India, we always have the Guru and the family elders to turn to. Many working mothers are also in close touch with their children's school teachers, so that their children's behaviour is carefully watched.

All of these offer excellent 'support systems' that can help parents monitor their children's behaviour during the crucial period of adolescence, and also to check adverse influences at an early stage.

Here are a few things you can do to keep your teenager close to you:

Communicate with your child regularly, systematically and openly.

When sixteen year old Babloo returns home at about 9.15 p.m. after his Maths coaching class, his Tennis practice and 'catching up' with friends, his parents are absorbed in their favourite TV serials. His mother Hema gets up during the commercial break, heats his food in the microwave and lays his plate on the table. By the time Babloo has washed, changed and sat down to dinner, she is 'lost' in her serial. Babloo eats his dinner, picks up the cordless phone and shuts himself up in his room.

At 10.30 p.m., when the parents are about to retire, they 'drop into' his room. When they enter, Babloo cuts off his phone-call. "How was the Maths Class today? his mother asks. "We had a surprise test," Babloo replies, "and I have done quite well." "Are you able to keep up with your tennis practice?" asks the father. "If you are not able to go regularly, do let me know. We are paying a fortune every month at the Tennis Academy."

"Don't worry Dad," says Babloo coldly. "No one's wasting your money. You can check at the Academy, I haven't missed a single day's coaching."

"Don't keep talking on the phone at all hours," scolds his mother. "Last month, the phone bill was over three thousand rupees. I certainly didn't talk that much!"

"Here, you can have your phone," Babloo retorts, holding out the cordless phone.

"Good boy," smiles the mother, not aware of his anger and resentment. "Now go to sleep, good night!"

This is hardly meaningful communication. Words have certainly been exchanged—but not to much purpose!

Happy, well-adjusted families will tell you that they constantly have family discussions and family-talk about major and minor issues that involve teenage children. Teenagers are very keen on their 'independence'; but they welcome parental approval and support for their ideas. Allow your teenager to express his opinions, wishes and aspirations; by all means offer him your valuable advice and suggestions; but do not impose your views on him rigidly.

As teenagers grow up, they are faced with new challenges, new problems and a few tough decisions. They have valuable inputs from their school, their teachers and their friends. Let us admit, children are more likely to be influenced by these views, rather than their parents' advice. Parents must not make the mistake of belittling these influences; they should talk about it with an open mind and help the children make the right choice.

Don't let conversations become conflicts !

Family discussions are good, but needless arguments can cause hostility and resentment in your teenager.

The Dutt family is plunged in gloom as their son Hari has failed to secure an engineering seat. They had been certain that he would get a seat at least in one of the rural colleges, but it is not to be.

Hari's parents are worried and anxious; but Hari himself is even more concerned. He has been talking to his friends, their elder brothers, his teachers and his uncle, whom he has always liked and admired. Based on their suggestions, he now tries to reassure himself and his parents.

"It's OK, Mama and Papa," he says bravely. "I will join B.Com. or B.A. in one of the local colleges. Sachin says he is joining NIIT for a Diploma in Software. I will do that too, so I get an added qualification. And then in the third year, Shah Sir says I can join coaching classes to prepare for MBA..."

"Since when has your friend Sachin become a counselor?" asks his father sarcastically. "He is hardly an expert that we should listen to his valuable advice!"

Hari flinches at the insult, but his mother adds her bit now.

"If Sachin imagines that NIIT comes cheap, ask him to think again," she chips in. "It costs a fortune – and who is to say that you will pass out? Mrs. Joshi's son gave up the course halfway because he could not cope."

Hari's anger begins to mount, when his father adds sourly, "And don't forget, if you could not clear the Engineering Entrance exams, what makes you sure that you can get into a good Management Institute? Or do you plan to turn brilliant and industrious in two years' time?"

The stage is all set for Hari to bark a nasty reply and start a slinging match with his parents. But let us skip this harsh scenario and 'rewrite' the whole situation.

"I can't believe I haven't made it Papa," Hari says, swinging between despair and apology. "I did my best in the entrance exams and I was pretty sure I would get Mechanical, if not Electronics."

"We know you tried your best son," his father tells him reassuringly. "But God has willed something else! However, there is no need to feel discouraged. It is not as if you belong to my generation, when the only choice was between Engineering and Medicine."

"Papa is right Hari," says his mother, squeezing his hands for support. "We are reading about so many exciting new options these days. Have you spoken to your friends who have opted out of Engineering? What are they planning to do?"

"Oh well, they have so many ideas Mom, that my head is reeling even to hear them out," Hari confesses. "I am not at all sure whether I want to try something wildly, as some of them are planning to do!"

"Why don't we take an appointment for you from a professional career counseling center?" the father observes. "You can meet with experts there; they will give you an aptitude test and also tell you about new courses that are available now."

"Can you really do that Dad?" asks Hari, cheering up. Then he adds, doubtfully, "Do you really think it will help?"

"We can always give it a try," says his father reassuringly. "Don't look so glum *beta*," he laughs, "it is not the end of the road, you know."

"I will ring up my cousin Sharada in Chennai," adds his mother. "You know she is the Principal of a well-known college there. I am sure she will also have some suggestions for you!"

The atmosphere has now improved considerably, and Hari is feeling far more optimistic. Of course, his parents are concerned about his future, but their first task is to see that their son is not demoralised by this setback, and to offer him the support and encouragement that he needs to revive his spirit and get on with his future.

Parents of teenagers should take care not to be harsh and judgmental about their children. Raising your voice, calling names and insulting will not get you very far! Respect your teenager's right to disagree with you; win him over by persuasion, rather than by coercion.

Avoid arguments especially when the situation is volatile and tempers are flaring. It is better to wait till everyone's anger has subsided, and you and your teenager are ready to sit down and sort out your differences. Shouting is not going to be of much help either!

Listen to your teenager!

Listening to your children carefully, letting them express their ideas and appreciating their view point is very important, if you wish to nurture your relationship.

I am afraid many parents today simply do not have the time to talk to their teenagers—leave alone listening to them patiently. Fathers plead pressure at the workplace or tensions in business; mothers complain that their hands are full with their home-making responsibilities. I would appeal to these busy couples—spare time to really listen to your children. Allow them to express themselves freely; just allow them to talk to you—without interrupting them to offer your advice or suggestions. Let them have their say—before you have yours!

Spend leisure hours with your children.

Plan recreational activities with them—it may be playing board games like Scrabble or Monopoly; it may be going out for a long leisurely walk; or an outing to a park or a museum; or just taking the family out for a drive—such activities help you get close to your teenagers and improves the quality of your relationship with them.

A young Rabbi and his wife were working hard to extend their kitchen so as to make it more modern and comfortable for the family. With three growing children to feed, money was short, and the Rabbi was not highly paid. His wife took on a few odd jobs to earn a few extra dollars, and both had their hands full with the Do-It-Yourself kits—for they could not afford to hire professional help.

"Papa, Papa, take us out trekking this weekend," begged the eldest son. "Our teacher said the hills are beautiful in the Fall, and rare birds come to the mountain springs now."

"Alright," agreed the Rabbi cheerfully. "We shall go trekking this weekend."

Later, as they cleared the kitchen table, the Rabbi's wife said to him, "Why did you have to commit yourself to the kids? We could have put up all the remaining shelves if we had worked through Sunday!"

The Rabbi smiled and said to her, "Honey, twenty, thirty years from now, our children will hardly remember our hard labour to put in the new extension to the kitchen. But believe me, they will remember their trek and the sights they saw and the fun they had! The things that interest us do not always interest our children. We must make it a point to do what *they* like every now and then. How else can we show them that we really care for them and love them?"

Value the leisure hours you spend with your children. Do not make it a sort of ritual that you go through mechanically—rather, plan and choose your recreation activities wisely so that it enhances the children's creativity, as well as their emotional and intellectual development.

Mrs. Sharma has a passion for visiting temples. If she gets so much as half a day off, she would like to jump into a car with her husband and teenage daughter and take off to the nearest place of worship. Long weekends and vacations are filled with even more temple visits.

Early on in this temple visiting spree, Mr. Sharma had noticed that their young daughter Reena, wasn't wildly excited about spending all her holidays at temples. He didn't blame her either—for he wasn't greatly interested in temples himself. Father and daughter hit on an excellent scheme: they would take Mrs. Sharma to the temple of her choice, and while she did her *parikramas* and *poojas* and joined the queue for repeated *darshan*, they would happily take off to explore the neighbourhood. When Reena was fifteen, she began to develop a keen interest in architecture— and the temple visits became even more attractive for the duo. Mrs. Sharma could spend hours inside— father and daughter had no complaints as they explored nooks and corners and discussed Hoysala architecture and Vijayanagar influences, sculpture and relief work, frescos and inlays.

The temple visits had truly become family outings!

Such regular, constructive outings lead to healthy, happy interaction between parents and children. They promote warmth and understanding among family members thus laying the foundation for a strong and secure bonding between parents and children.

When you plan your holidays, take the children into your confidence and ask them what kind of vacation they would prefer. Try and accommodate their interests to the best possible extent. This will give them the added satisfaction that their parents listen to them, care for their interests and are ready to do what *they* want!

When you spend happy leisure hours together, your relationship with your children improves, bringing greater warmth and comfort all around. Should the need for strict discipline or corrective action arise later on, the strong bonds you have developed will stand you in good stead.

Don't interfere with your teenagers personal tastes, by fussing about minor issues that are really not crucial.

Many parents may not agree with this, but to my mind, such irrelevant issues which you can leave to your children's discretion include the following:

- their chosen hairstyle
- the organization / decoration of their room
- their choice of clothes
- their choice of food and music

Let me hasten to add, there are issues on which parents *must* have the final word—such as safety in the home and on the road, dating, driving the family car and the amount of pocket money given to children.

When you allow children to choose what they like and make their own decisions in certain matters, you help them to develop independence and develop self-confidence and security.

I would even urge you to go one step further, and invite your teenagers to contribute to certain family decisions—like planning a holiday or a party, visiting friends/relatives, redecorating the home, etc. It boosts the children's morale to know that their views are respected, and that they can help you to arrive at decisions.

Therefore, do not make a habit of constantly interfering with your teenager's life in negligible, unimportant issues. Save your energy and your concern for more important things where your guidance is vital. Equally, allow your teenager to express his opinion on matters concerning the family, so that he may grow in self-confidence and maturity.

Mr. Gupta had been told that his company would be giving him a new car. He was, naturally, delighted. But there was a dilemma. The company had given him a choice between two brand new models of different motor companies that had been introduced into the market. Both looked equally attractive, both brands enjoyed equal reputation.

Mr. Gupta knew what he was going to do. That evening when he went home, he went straight to his son's room. Fifteen year old Praveen was standing on his bed and playing his guitar, imitating the rock star who was singing on his TV screen. The room was in a mess, with clothes strewn all over, and CDs lying open, and wires from the guitar and the music system and the computer criss-crossing all available space.

Mr. Gupta stood at the door and waved to his son. "Hi there!" he called. "Is there any way I can actually get into this room without falling over?"

"Oh, Hi Dad!" called Praveen, hastily divesting himself of the guitar and its wires, and clearing the rest of the stuff so that his father could walk in.

"Rolling Stones, eh?" the father remarked, looking at the TV screen. "Did you know they were around when I was your age!"

"Don't say!" marveled Praveen. "They have certainly stood the test of time, haven't they, Dad?"

Father and son settled down and Mr. Gupta said to Praveen, "I am getting a new car from the company."

Praveen was ecstatic. He did a victory dance, leapt up on the bed and generally expressed his joy like a typical teenager.

"But you have got to do some work for me," Mr. Gupta continued. "I want you to go on the Net, visit the car users' websites and tell me which car we should choose, because, frankly, my friends and I cannot make up our minds."

"Leave it to me Dad," Praveen assured him enthusiastically. "The trick is to avoid conventional websites which are only used for publicity. We will go to the blogs and post queries—that's where the genuine users are, and that's where we will get the information we need. I am getting on to the computer right away!"

When Mr. Gupta had stood at his son's door, he could have started off by criticizing the noise, the mess in the room and Praveen's antics on the bed. True, Praveen needed to be told to be neat and orderly— but at that point, these were really minor, irrelevant issues. Mr. Gupta wisely ignored them and treated his son as an adult and equal, calling for his contribution to the decision of choosing a car. Praveen felt wonderful, and in a matter of hours, he had looked up multiple websites and gathered so much information, including complaints from the owners and problems identified by them, and actually made a systematic list of pros and cons for each car. That was not all; when he asked his father to come over to his room to view the 'results' on his computer, he had cleaned up his room, and was actually able to offer Mr. Gupta a chair on which there were no belts, no jeans, no books!

Help your teenagers to develop morals and values—not by lecturing to them or enforcing rules on them, but by making them aware of what is right and wrong, and about acceptable and unacceptable behaviour.

This is easier said than done! But you can inculcate values in the children by

1. Being affectionate, caring parents—but also firm and fair minded at the same time.
2. By laying down rules that are consistent and clear—not confusing and contradictory.
3. Allowing them to take responsibility for decision-making and leadership wherever possible.
4. Asking for their help and contribution in family events and community activities.
5. Talking to children about society, politics, religion and spirituality in a way that appeals to them. For instance, a recent event or development could be discussed by the family, so that children draw the right lessons from the same.

6. Encouraging children to express their choices and attitudes to these issues, and trying to understand their reasons for their opinions.
7. Involving the children in constructive community activities such as social service, peace rallies and public discourses by eminent spiritual leaders so that they are exposed to a broader, more selfless view of life.
8. Making them responsible and accountable for their actions, and helping them to realize the consequences of their own actions. If they have made a wrong decision or a poor choice, they must be held accountable, and allowed to experience the bad effects, so that they take the corrective measures in a spirit of awareness and understanding.
9. Being good, fair, consistent parents—rather than trying to spoil your child, and doing all you can to win his favour. Your role is to be a true friend, guide and guardian to the youngster—not someone who wants to please them and win a popularity contest.
10. Practising what you preach. I have said earlier, children learn far more from your life and your behaviour, than from your verbal instructions.

Parenting is not only one of the greatest pleasures of your life – it is also an onerous responsibility, involving psychology, ethics, human resource management, spirituality, morals and religion. Whatever I have outlined above are not to be taken as rigid rules, but they can help you adopt your own parenting style towards your teenager.

Let me conclude by saying that your teenagers look up to you for a sense of security, identity and belonging. The world we live in is changing as fast, that they are exposed to powerful, sometimes negative influences from outside. The only weapon with which you have to fight these negative influences is your love – therefore, make your teenager feel loved, cherished and secure! Express your love in as many ways as you can, as often as you can. Let your discipline and control become expressions of your love and concern – rather than being merely negative feedback and criticism. Give them your unstinted praise and appreciation when they deserve it. Treat them as young adults and as responsible members of the family unit. You will find that your children bloom and flower into mature, sensible adults under your loving care!

How To Deal With Teenagers' Problems

As we have seen, a well-balanced, well-ordered, happy, wholesome family atmosphere is crucial for the emotional and intellectual development of the children. Experts say that when the home 'structure' is out of balance – i.e. when it is too rigid or too lax – it may result in oppositional or negative behaviour traits.

Some parents are inflexible and harsh about rules; they come down heavily on the children for the least mistake. They become obsessed with controlling every aspect of the child's life – what he wears, what he eats, the friends he chooses, even his leisure activities and interests.

This attitude can only create resentment and defiance in teenagers. On the other hand, a completely 'loose' structure is also to be avoided – where the parents' attitude is lax, where no clear rules and boundaries are laid down, and children are allowed to come and go as they please. In such conditions, parents give in to all their children's demands – either because they are eager to please, or out of a misplaced desire to avoid 'unpleasantness'.

Neither of these extremes is desirable. What parents must cultivate is a loving but firm attitude, a balanced structure in which they retain their authority, while the children feel loved, protected and secure; where they realize that rules are meant to ensure their wellbeing and safety – and above all, their bright and happy future.

Sadly, sometimes, parents disagree with each other on crucial parenting issues. The wife feels that the children must be given a lavish allowance, allowed to cultivate an extravagant lifestyle and adopt a social life that includes parties, clubs, picnics, dances and movies. The husband, who has risen in life through his own painstaking efforts, believes that his children should learn the value of money and live an austere life without added frills and luxuries. When the couple fail to agree on such issues, it creates a confusing situation for the children.

Parents must also be warned, that when there is inconsistency in the rules they impose, children are likely to choose the lax set of rules – or even to set up one parent against another.

Janice has fared very poorly in her Eleventh standard exam. To enforce greater discipline on her,

her father, Mr. D'Souza, has laid down the rule that she will stay at home and devote herself to her studies every evening from six to nine. Although Janice is annoyed by this 'condition', she decides to use this to her advantage against her mother. Mrs. D'Souza is an Accountant in a multinational, and when she gets home around 7 p.m., she relies on a lot of help from her daughter to get dinner ready. Now, Janice has the perfect excuse *not* to help her mother: "Papa has said I must not leave my study-table between six and nine!"

Mrs. D'Souza is tired and upset. "You're making her lazy and selfish," she accuses her husband. "What is more important, her studies or your kitchen work?" demands her husband angrily. Janice watches them argue from the sidelines, delighted that the focus is not on her poor performance.

My appeal to parents is this: if you do have disagreements, attempt to resolve them *in the absence of your children*. After all, when you are setting rules for children, you must practise what you preach!

When teenagers become aggressive and rude, it is no use screaming or shouting at them! Tough as it may sound, parents must remain calm, and order the child to keep quiet, or walk out of an explosive situation to 'take time out'. Appropriate boundaries must be set for children's behaviour – and if they misbehave, they must face the consequences of their own action.

Experts tell us that one of the reasons why teenagers take to aggression and rebellion is that the 'child' is trying to grow up too quickly and assume the role of an adult. For whatever reason they begin to think that they are 'equal' to their parents, and can 'stand up' to them. Unfortunately, such conflicts also make them feel less loved, less wanted and less cherished. Parents are only too ready to soothe them and reassure them of their love – but this pushes them back (so they feel) into the role of 'children' and they resent this. We have to understand that it is extremely difficult to operate as an adult and still crave love and protection as a child. Parents must therefore learn the difficult art of combining love and affection with the ability to soothe the child's anxiety and frustration – even when the child displays negative behaviour patterns.

Look out for warning signals in the teenager's behaviour such as:

- Agitated or restless behaviour and mood swings
- Sudden loss or gain in weight
- Drop in school grades
- Depression, sullenness
- Avoiding the company of family members
- Lack of motivation and enthusiasm
- Lethargy, exhaustion and loss of interest in daily routine
- Rise in 'inferiority complex' and a feeling of worthlessness

What do these signals tell us, you may ask. The opinion of experts may seem exaggerated – but they say these are indications of problems varying from common eating disorders to serious habits like drug abuse.

Let me hasten to assure you, there are hundreds of thousands of teenagers who are growing up happily in families like yours, *without* such serious problems. Every parent has had to cope with the occasional act of disobedience, defiance of rules and preferences for friends over family. What they must look out for is when such behaviour patterns become frequent and repetitive.

If you do suspect that there is a problem, talk to your teenagers; encourage them to tell you what is bothering them – and listen to them when they talk! Don't interrupt their crucial communication with your comments and suggestions.

Let me urge you *not* to ignore problems – it is far easier to deal with problems when they are small.

If none of this works, do turn to people for help – to the children's teachers, to their grandparents, to your family doctor – and above all, to your *guru*.

Nowadays, educational psychologists and counselors are available at good schools and they can also offer you valuable insights on educational and relationship issues.

Grown-up children must be taught, too, that 'freedom' must not become 'license' – especially in their relationship with members of the opposite sex. In this, as in all else, let the children remember that they must do *nothing* that will bring shame on their family, especially their parents.

Often, young boys and girls leaving home for higher studies – to go abroad, or to go far away from their home town – come to say goodbye to me; some of them ask me for a few words of counsel which they can carry with them in their hearts. This is what I always tell them:

"*Never, ever* do anything for which your parents will be ashamed of you!"

Some of them have told me that those words have truly helped them in crucial moments!

Now, The Good News!

"Adolescence" says an expert, "has had a bad press." This is perhaps true; many teenagers 'bloom' into admirable adults, putting problems behind them, and evolving through many positive changes – changes for the better!

Difficult times come and go for all of us – don't you remember the challenges and obstacles you faced as a teenager? Think of the growing-up 'pains' you faced then – and you will be able to emphathise with your children and support them as they evolve into adulthood. And remember too, that with each passing week, month and year, the problems of the past are being put behind, forever!

Remember too, the anxiety and concern that you experience is more than matched by the turmoil and unhappiness that your children are passing through. You are in it together – and together, you will come out of it whole! Your children will grow up to be mature, responsible young adults– and you will experience the profound satisfaction of having helped them through their most difficult years!

FAQs – Parents & Children

Q1.: Can you offer some practical suggestions to parents desirous of bringing up their children in the right way?

Ans.: Here are a few tips which may be found helpful:

1. There is a difference between children and adults. Children live in the now; they are free from anxieties of the past and fear of the future. If a child is in need of something or wants an answer to a question, never say to him, "I shall fulfill your need or answer your question tomorrow or at my leisure."

2. Every child is a human being, with a heart and soul. Never let him feel that he is too small to make any constructive suggestions for the good of the family. How true it is, that sometimes, God speaks through the mouth of babes. Listen to what he has to say, and appreciate his suggestions. And never forget that the child is an individual, with his own personality and innate talents. Understand him and encourage the creative principle within him to express itself freely. Guide him in a healthy, constructive way by bringing out the best that is

in him. Do not impose your will on him and say, "I am a doctor, so my son should become a doctor!"

3. In your treatment towards children, do not discriminate. Do not let them feel that a particular child is your favourite. Children are very sensitive creatures.

4. Keep your child very close to yourself, until he is at least three years of age. He needs your affectionate touch. It is a great blunder to hand over little children to *ayahs* or baby-sitters.

5. It sometimes becomes very necessary to scold children. Whenever you do so, avoid being emotional. Let your words on such occasions be like whips of love. Explain the fault clearly to the child, and allow him to speak out, if he has anything to say. And please, after you have scolded your child, and he has regretted his mistake, forget all about it — and continue to be the loving parent that you always are.

6. Even at a young age, children should be trained to attend to household chores. Let them cultivate reverence for manual work and permit them to feel proud of having contributed their little bit to the common good.

7. Let children grow in a spirit of unselfishness by training them to share food with the starving ones. Sri Krishna says in the Gita, "He who cooks for himself alone, is a thief!" Before you eat your food, set apart a share for a hungry one – a man, a bird, or an animal. Example is always a better teacher than precept.

8. The home is a door to the Kingdom of God, the kingdom of true happiness. Let all the members

of the family gather together, at a prayer meeting – even if it be for ten to fifteen minutes. This will give a new tone to the home. At a prominent place in your hone, keep a big, beautiful picture of some great one – Krishna or Rama, Buddha or Jesus, Zoroaster or Guru Nanak, Mira or Mahavir, Baha'u'llah or Kabir or a saint of humanity – to whom you feel drawn. Whenever you or the children leave the house or enter it, bow down to the picture and offer a small prayer.

Q2: In families today, parents discipline their children by scolding them and punishing them. They use expressions like, "*Bad* behaviour, *bad* girl, *bad* boy" in the hope of changing their behaviour. Is there an alternative?

Ans.: The alternative is that we must give more time and more attention to our children. And we must give them the pure, selfless love of the heart. We have denied these three things to our children. The truth of the matter is that no child can grow in the right way without love. Today, for the sake of convenience, we have handed the children over to the TV screen. The TV shows them many good things that they should see, but also things they should not see.

Interestingly, it takes longer for the good things to have an effect on the mind of the child, while negative things have an immediate effect in influencing his character. Parents today are busy making money. When I ask them, "Why are you making money?" They answer, "We are making money for our children." But, in the bargain, they lose their children because they don't give them time, attention, and the love of their hearts.

It is better to leave them with an understanding heart than with tons of money.

Q3: Are parents to be blamed for neglecting their children?

Ans.: Not many parents seem to realise their responsibilities towards the children. It was William Tame who said, "Men are generally more careful about the breed of their horses and dogs than their own children."

Of Plato, the great Greek philosopher, it is said that when he found a child doing wrong, he went and corrected the father for it.

Q4: Dadaji, how could we make the generation gap a pleasant experience?

Ans.: The difficulty with the young people, and I too regard myself as one of them, is that we think that we have mastered the knowledge and wisdom of the whole world. We carry it on the palm of our hands. If only we realise that our parents have passed through many experiences and gathered wisdom from which we can learn, this generation gap will not be a problem. It is because the children feel that their parents don't understand them and do not know anything, that the generation gap is created.

I believe, it is the duty of the parent to become friends with their children when they are in their teens. In their teens, young boys and girls need friends more than parents. The parent must show interest in every detail of the teenagers' life so that he or she does not hesitate in confiding everything in the parent. The teenager is in search of a true friend who, even though he knows his faults and failings, yet loves him and understands him.

In our days, there was no generation gap at all. We never heard the word, generation gap. We hear of it now. Why? Because in our days, all of the mother's time, her energies, her attention, were devoted to the upbringing of the children. Today, so many mothers have to go and earn. They are absent from the house for many hours at a stretch. Or, those who do not have the necessity to earn, go to clubs. They neglect their children which creates this generation gap.

In our days, there was no generation gap. And no one taught us not to smoke, not to eat meat, not to drink wine! We were brought up in that atmosphere, therefore, it became natural for us. Till today I have never smoked! It was not because I was told not to smoke but because we were in that atmosphere.

The best discipline is self-discipline. Unless you have self-discipline, unless you have self-control, you cannot lead a disciplined life.

The father says to the boy, "You must not smoke," but he himself turns round and smokes. The boy sees the father smoking and says, "He tells me not to smoke and he is enjoying himself. I will also enjoy myself." The boy also turns round and starts smoking. Examples speak louder than words.

Q5: Dadaji, what is the difference between today's generation and yesterday's generation?
Ans.: The difference between today's generation and yesterday's generation is only the difference that is between today and yesterday. Your question contains

the answer. But if you ask me, what is it that today's generation needs? I will give the answer in one word – reverence, which is the root of knowledge. Without reverence, there can be no true education, there can be no true knowledge.

That is why the great English poet said, "Let knowledge grow from more to more, but more of reverence in us dwell." We are becoming more and more irreverent today. Yesterday's generation had greater reverence for their parents, their elders, their teachers and for the one indefinable Mystery, which, for want of a better word, we call God.

Reverence is of three types. Reverence for what is above us, reverence for what is around us and what is beneath us. Reverence for the poor, the broken ones, the blind, the handicapped, and reverence for birds and animals, who, too, are our brothers and sisters in the one family of creation. If only this reverence could enter our hearts, the world would become new.

Q6: Dada, why don't parents allow their children to date?

Ans.: Let me answer your question by telling you of a conversation I heard between a girl and her mother.

The girl asked her mother, "Mommy, may I go out this evening with my boyfriend?"

"No, my child," said the mother.

"Why, Mommy, don't you trust me?"

"I do trust you, my child," said the mother.

"Then, don't you trust my boyfriend?"

"I do trust him," the mother said.

"Then what is the reason?" asked the girl.

And the mother said, "I don't trust the two of you together."

Q7:How can we accept our parents' views when ours are different? Sometimes we simply cannot agree. What do we do when this happens?

Ans.: There is a great man who observed, "When I was twenty, I felt that my parents were foolish and that I knew everything and they knew nothing. At the age of thirty, I began to see that there was some little wisdom in what my parents said. At the age of forty, I found that there was not a little, but quite a lot of wisdom and common sense in all that they said. At the age of fifty, I have realized that I was a fool to have disregarded what my parents told me."

It is true that there are many points on which youth disagree with adults, especially in this age, which is a transitional period. Values are changing. The values of the older generation are quite different from those of the new generation. One thing, which I feel can help, is to put yourself in the place of your parents. I do not ask you to accept everything that your parents tell you. May be your parents do not understand the problems you face. But you must put yourself in their place and consider what your condition would be if your children behaved towards you as you are behaving towards your parents.

Second, the parents should grow in patience. I tell parents, again and again, that they should be friends to their children. They must be easily accessible to the children so that the children will never hesitate to tell them anything. What is happening now is that the children try to hide many things from their parents, which is wrong. This will cut at the very roots of family life.

Let me repeat, when a child grows to be a teenager, parents must become his friends. The attitude of parents and children alike needs to change. Children should be more respectful to their parents. Parents must be more understanding with regard to children's problems. It is only then, that we will be able to build up a happy family life once again. As it is, I am afraid that the gulf between children and parents is widening.

Thirdly, also try to explain to yourself that your parents have passed through their own teenage phase and they have also had to face similar problems. They can give you the right advice. Therefore, listen to them. Think over what they tell you and then do what you consider to be right.

Q8: Why are mothers always right?

Ans.: It is only for the sake of expediency that we claim that mothers are always right – not from the absolute point of view!

I once visited an office. On each one of the desks at which the workers sat, there was a small placard which said: "The boss is always right."

I do not think that this is right in a family. It may be right in an industry or an organization. If I think the boss is not right I can leave the organization and go and join another. But a family is a family, you cannot leave it and join another family. There should be a more flexible attitude, a give and take arrangement.

Q9: Dadaji, in spite of guidance, advice and suggestions from parents, why is it that youngsters today, do not follow the path of truth sincerely?

Ans.: Why? It is for the young people to answer. One of the reasons perhaps, is that whatever is told to them, they do not take seriously.

Another reason is because the parents themselves do not bear witness in deeds of daily living to the teachings they would wish to pass on to their children. Every parent should be a model, a perfect example of the teaching that he/she wishes to pass on to the child. Children do not learn through words, they learn through life.

What kind of life are the parents living? If the mother and the father are quarrelling with each other all the time, and they tell the child not to quarrel with anyone, how will the child understand?

If you practise this type of duplicity, what is the child going to do? That is the great difficulty. Today our parents are placing before their children ideals to which their lives do not bear witness. This is why many children are disillusioned.

Q10: How can we develop friendship with our children?

Ans.: To develop friendship with your children you must:

1. Start early. Don't wait until they become teenagers. Then it will be too late.
2. The first time your children meet you in the morning or when they return from school, greet them warmly. Press their arm; give them a hug or

a kiss to assure them that they are important to you.

3. Develop close proximity with your children till they are three years old. At that tender age, they need your affectionate touch and your warm response to everything they do or say.

4. Be a good listener. When the child is talking to you, give him your full attention. Do not dismiss him summarily. Listen to him patiently. Every child wants an interested ear.

5. Try to understand your child. No child expects his parents to agree with him all the time, but he has a right to be understood.

6. Do not humiliate your children, especially in the presence of their peers.

7. Don't let down the trust of a child, especially if he trusts you with a secret, regard it as sacred.

8. To deal with your children in the right way, you need to cultivate a rich sense of humour.

9. Meal times should be times of coming closer to each other. The TV should be switched off.

10. If you want to make friends with your children, you must know their friends.

11. Do not discriminate among children. Let them not have a feeling that one of them is your favourite.

12. Children should be encouraged to help with domestic chores, especially at an early age. This gives them a sense of belonging, a sense of contribution to the family.

13. Don't create fantasies about your child's future according to your own expectations and desires.

We must not regard our children as an extension of our hopes and dreams.

14. Encourage the children to share food with the starving ones – human beings, birds and animals.

15. Remember, a home is a door to the Kingdom of God. Everyday, at an appointed hour, all the members of the family, young and old, must get together at a prayer meeting. This will create a new atmosphere of love and harmony and peace in every house. The family that prays together, stays together.